New Edition

A Shortcut to Cantonese

An innovative approach for English and Putonghua speakers

Yin-Ping Cream Lee
Shin Kataoka

Greenwood Press

GREENWOOD PRESS
802 & 804 Golden Industrial Building,
16-26 Kwai Tak Street, Kwai Chung,
New Territories.
Tel: (852) 2546 8212, 25477 041
Fax: (852) 2858 6042
Email: gwpress@ctimail.com
Website: www.green-woodpress.com

First published April, 2013

ISBN 978-962-279-293-7

PRINTED IN HONG KONG

Yin Ping Cream Lee dedicates this book to her mother with love
Lai Mo Lin

李燕萍將此書獻給她摯愛的母親
黎慕蓮

Acknowledgements

We thank Lan Fu for her valuable feedback on an earlier draft of this book. We are also indebted to Ricky Sham for reading the final manuscript and providing professional comments and suggestions. Nevertheless we are of course responsible for any remaining shortcomings.

We would also like to express our gratitude to Ricky Sham and Kitty Leung for their lively recordings.

Contents

How to use this book

◇◇◇◇◇◇◇◇◇◇◇◇◇◇◇◇◇◇◇◇◇◇◇◇◇◇◇◇◇◇◇◇◇◇◇

Who is this book for?

This book is designed for learners who want to learn Cantonese in a lively way. Since this book is primarily designed for those who know Chinese, native Putonghua speakers and learners with prior knowledge of Putonghua will find this book extremely useful to learn Cantonese.

How is this book different from other Cantonese textbooks?

A lot of learners of Cantonese speak Putonghua as their mother tongue or have prior knowledge of Putonghua. To make the most of their knowledge of pronunciations and grammar rules in Putonghua, corresponding words in Putonghua are given and brief comparison is made in each chapter of this book. This is why this book is so unique and different from other types of Cantonese textbooks.

How shall I use this book?

Every chapter can be effectively learned if you …

1. Listen to the native Cantonese speakers' conversation recorded in the attached CD-ROM and try to mimic them.
2. Try to meet the learning tasks of each chapter by going through vocabulary lists, practicing dialogues and reading grammar notes.
3. Grasp the similarities and differences between Cantonese and Putonghua with the explanatory notes in this book, while trying to avoid interference from Putonghua.

Which Cantonese Romanized System is used in this book?

The system called 'Jyutping' is employed in this book. Learners with prior knowledge of Putonghua are usually familiar with 'Hanyu Pinyin'. Since 'Jyutping' is similar to 'Hanyu Pinyin'(for instance, both systems use'z, c, s'), learners should find it easy to master 'Jyutping'. Tones are denoted by numbers in this system. In order to make pitch contour easy to remember, we created a tone-embedded numerical sign, which you find on top of every other page.

Since an increasing number of Cantonese learning aids such as dictionaries and textbooks have come out in this system, the mastery of 'Jyutping' will enable you to access to other useful materials. A bonus point is that 'Jyutping' is one of the bundled input methods for Office applications in Windows, so you can type Chinese characters with it.

Some Cantonese sounds are difficult. How can I master them?

Each chapter focuses on some features of Cantonese sounds and tones that English and Putonghua speakers may find difficult. In case there are similar sounds, minimal pairs are provided in order for learners to grasp the differences. Try to pronounce those sounds as instructed.

Is there more to learn?

Sure! To help you increase your word power, supplementary vocabulary related to the theme is provided in each chapter.

Is there any exercise?

Yes! To help you consolidate what you have learned, exercises are provided in each chapter. Answer keys are provided in order to check how well you have done.

About Cantonese

◇◇◇◇◇◇◇◇◇◇◇◇◇◇◇◇◇◇◇◇◇◇◇◇◇◇◇◇

Cantonese is a spoken variety of Chinese with some 70 million speakers. It is a language widely spoken in the Guangdong province of China and is the dominant language spoken in Hong Kong and Macau. Since Guangdong is one of the main homelands of overseas Chinese, Cantonese is also spoken in Chinatowns worldwide. If you live in Hong Kong, you will realize many Cantonese-related loanwords are used in Hong Kong English, such as "**dim sum**" (*Cantonese style food served on small plates*), "**kung fu**" (*martial arts*), "**Kung Hey Fat Choy**" (*a popular Chinese New Year blessing*) and so on. Since language is deeply related to culture, the mastery of Cantonese will help you understand Cantonese culture, especially Hong Kong culture.

Some of you have learned Putonghua before, and some of you are Putonghua native speakers. In the following section, we will give you a brief picture of how Cantonese and Putonghua, the two major spoken varieties of Chinese, differ in terms of pronunciation, vocabulary, and grammar.

Pronunciation

Initials

1. Cantonese has 19 initial consonants while Putonghua has 21.
2. Putonghua has three sets of consonants, namely "j, q, x", "z, c, s" and "zh, ch, sh". In comparison, Cantonese has only one set: "z, c, s".
3. Cantonese uses "ng" as a syllabic-initial consonant, such as "ngo" (first person pronoun), while Putonghua does not.
4. In Cantonese, "g" and "k" pronounced with round lips are classified as independent initials "gw" and "kw". The pronunciations of these, however, are similar to Putonghua "g" and "k" in front of a medial vowel "u".
5. Putonghua initials do not always correspond well with Cantonese initials.

Finals

1. Cantonese has 51 finals while Putonghua has 36.
2. Cantonese differentiates long and short vowels, such as "a", and "aa".
3. Cantonese has three nasal endings "-m/-n/-ng", and three plosive endings "-p/-t/-k", while Putonghua has only two nasal endings "-n/-ng" and no plosive endings.

4. Cantonese has round vowels such as "**eo**" and "**oe**", which Putonghua or English lacks. Similar vowels can be found in French or German.
5. Cantonese lacks medial vowels such as "**i**, **u**, **ü**" in Putonghua.
6. Putonghua finals do not always correspond to Cantonese finals.

Tones

1. Cantonese has **6** tones, while Putonghua has **4**. (The traditional classification divides the Cantonese tones into 9 kinds, but there are only 6 pitch patterns.)
2. There are 2 sets of tones in Cantonese: **high** and **low**, while there is no such distinction in Putonghua.
3. There is no neutral tone in Cantonese.
4. Putonghua tones do not always correspond to Cantonese tones.

Vocabulary

1. Same concepts may be expressed with different words in Cantonese and Putonghua. For example:

Cantonese	Putonghua	English
bei²（俾）	gěi（給）	*give*
sik⁶（食）	chī（吃）	*eat*

2. Some Cantonese monosyllabic words correspond to disyllabic words in Putonghua. For example:

Cantonese	Putonghua	English
kat¹（咳）	késou（咳嗽）	*to cough*
ngaan⁵（眼）	yǎnjing（眼睛）	*eye*

3. Cantonese uses more loanwords than Putonghua. For example:

Cantonese	Putonghua	English
seot¹ • saam¹（恤衫）	chènshān（襯衫）	*shirt*
si⁶ • do¹ • be¹ • lei²（士多啤梨）	cǎoméi（草莓）	*strawberry*

4. The Putonghua suffix “zi" does not exist in spoken Cantonese. For example:

Cantonese	Putonghua	English
fu³ (褲)	kùzi (褲子)	*pants*
toi²* (枱)	zhuōzi (桌子)	*table*

5. Words written alike in Cantonese and Putonghua may have different meanings. For example:

Characters	Putonghua	Cantonese
姑娘	gūniang (*young lady*)	gu¹ • noeng⁴ (*nurse*)
奶奶	nǎinai (*grandmother*)	naai⁴ • naai² (*husband's mother*)

6. Cantonese colloquial terms are often written with special characters, knows as dialectal characters, which are never used in Putonghua. For example:

Cantonese	Putonghua	English
keoi⁵ (佢)	tā (他)	*he / she / it*
hai² (喺)	zài (在)	*in / at*

7. Some Cantonese words are closely related to the Cantonese culture. For example:

7.1 Snow- and ice-related concepts are often expressed with “syut³” in Cantonese, whereas the same word only refers to snow-related concepts in Putonghua. For example, “syut³ • gwai⁶” (雪櫃 *refrigerator* / 冰箱 in Putonghua) , or “syut³ • gou¹” (雪糕 *ice cream* / 冰淇淋 in Putonghua) (雪糕), etc.

7.2 Cantonese words that sound inauspicious are replaced by those with auspicious meanings. For example, “hung¹” empty (空) is a homonym with “hung¹” evil (凶), so it is often replaced by “gat¹” (吉 *lucky*), as in “gat¹ • uk¹” (吉屋 *empty flat*).

Grammar

That all Chinese dialects share the same grammar is only a myth. Despite some similarities, Cantonese and Putonghua, in fact, have a lot of differences in grammar.

1. Demonstratives

In Cantonese, the combination of a classifier and a noun can be used without a demonstrative, which is ungrammatical in Putonghua. For example:

Cantonese	**Zi^{1} bat^{1} hai^{6} m^{4} hai^{6} nei^{5} gaa^{3}?**	**(枝筆係唔係你㗎)**	*correct*
Putonghua	* Zhī bǐ shì bushì nǐ de?	(支笔是不是你的？)	*wrong*
	Zhè zhī bǐ shì bushì nǐ de?	(这支笔是不是你的？)	*correct*
English	*Is the pen yours?*		

2. Word Order

In Cantonese, the direct object precedes the indirect object, whereas Putonghua takes the reverse order. For example:

Cantonese	**Keoi^{5} bei^{2} cin^{2*} ngo^{5}.**	**(佢俾錢我)**	*correct*
Putonghua	* Tā gěi qián wǒ.	(他给钱我)	*wrong*
	Tā gěi wǒ qián.	(他给我钱)	*correct*
English	*He gives me money.*		

3. Comparison Structure

In Cantonese, "gwo^{3} 過" is placed right after the adjective to introduce the object of comparison, whereas in Putonghua, the object of comparison is expressed after "bǐ 比", which is placed in front of the adjective. For example:

Cantonese	**Ngo^{5} hau^{6} • saang^{1} gwo^{3} keoi^{5}.**	**(我後生過佢)**
Putonghua	Wǒ bǐ tā niánqīng.	(我比他年轻)
English	*I am younger than he.*	

Cantonese romanization system

Cantonese is a tonal language, and its syllabic structure is very different from English.

A typical Cantonese syllable consists of three elements:

1. Initial: syllabic-initial consonant
2. Final: syllabic-final vowel (plus an ending consonant)
3. Tone: relative pitch of a syllable

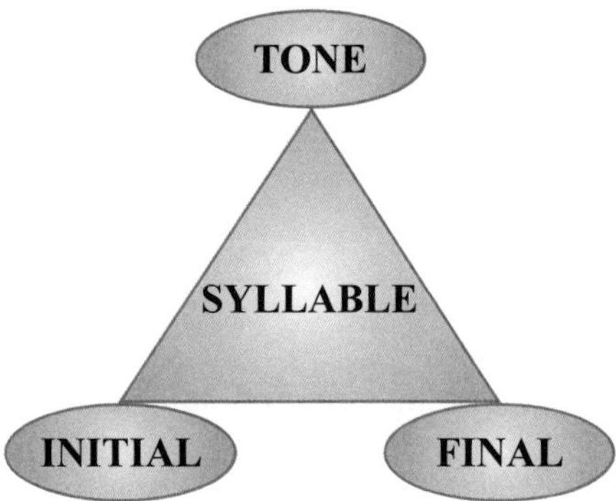

An example of a syllable is like this:

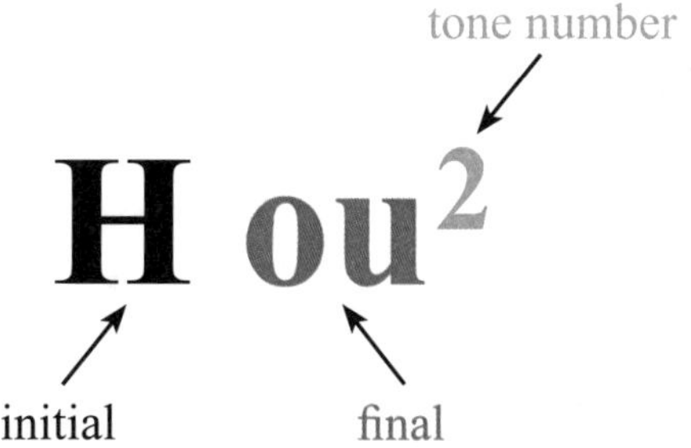

(Hou²: the Cantonese word for *good*)

Jyutping (粵拼)

The Cantonese romanization system employed in this book is called **Jyutping**, a system developed by the Linguistic Society of Hong Kong in 1993.

This romanization has been gaining ground not only in the materials for Cantonese learning, but also as the input method in computing and telecommunication system. An increasing number of textbooks, dictionaries, and e-learning materials have been published in Jyutping. This system also comes as one of the bundled Chinese input methods in Windows Office applications under the name of Hong Kong Cantonese. Unlike other systems, one letter in Jyutping basically denotes only one sound. All these factors make us believe that learners will benefit most from this system.

In the following section, we will briefly illustrate how Jyutping is used to denote Cantonese initials, finals and tones.

1. Initials

Remember that 'gw', 'kw', and 'ng' are pronounced as one consonant.

Table 1 Cantonese initials *(Track 001)*

Initials	Romanization & Chinese characters		English Meaning
Aspirated:			
p	paa^1	趴	*crouch down*
t	taa^1	他	*he*
k	kaa^1	卡	*card*
c	caa^1	叉	*fork*
kw	$kwaa^1$	誇	*boast*
Unaspirated:			
b	baa^1	爸	*father*
d	daa^1	打	*dozen*
g	gaa^1	家	*family*
z	zaa^1	渣	*dregs*
gw	$gwaa^1$	瓜	*melon*
Nasal			
m	maa^1	媽	*mother*
n	naa^1		
ng	$ngaa^1$	鴉	*crow*

Fricative & Continuant			
f	faa[1]	花	*flower*
l	laa[1]	啦	*final particle*
h	haa[1]	蝦	*shrimp*
s	saa[1]	沙	*sand*
Semi-Vowel			
j	jaa[1]	吔	*interjection*
w	waa[1]	娃	*baby*

†† Ngaa[1] is a colloquial pronunciation of 鴉 (standard form: aa[1]).

2. Finals :

Long and short vowels make a contrast in Cantonese. As you will see, Jyutping is so designed that the sound contrast can be mostly seen by the use of different letters.

Table 2 Cantonese finals *(Track 002)*

aa & a	aa (long 'a')				a (short 'a')			
	vowel (+ending)	example		English	vowel (+ending)	example		English
	a	zaa[3]	炸	*deep-fried*				
	aai	faai[3]	快	*fast*	**ai**	fai[3]	費	*expenses*
	aau	gaau[3]	教	*teach*	**au**	gau[3]	夠	*enough*
	aam	gaam[3]	鑑	*examine*	**am**	gam[3]	禁	*forbid*
	aan	jaan[3]	讚	*praise*	**an**	jan[3]	震	*shake*
	aang	saang[1]	生	*to be born*	**ang**	sang[1]	生	*life*
	aap	saap[3]	霎	*instant*	**ap**	sap[1]	濕	*wet*
	aat	baat[3]	八	*eight*	**at**	bat[1]	筆	*pen*
	aak	haak[3]	嚇	*intimidate*	**ak**	hak[1]	黑	*dark*

e	long				short			
	vowel (+ending)	example		English	vowel (+ending)	example		English
	e	ze[3]	借	*borrow*	**ei**	sei[3]	四	*four*
	eng	leng[3]	靚	*beautiful*				
	ek	tek[3]	踢	*kick*				

oe & eo	long oe			short eo		
	vowel (+ending)	example	English	vowel (+ending)	example	English
	oe	**hoe**^{1} 靴	*boot*	**eoi**	**heoi**^{1} 虛	*empty*
	oeng	**soeng**^{1} 商	*commerce*	**eon**	**seon**^{1} 詢	*inquire*
	oek	**zoek**^{3} 着	*wear*	**eot**	**ceot**^{1} 出	*out*

†† In colloquial speech, there exists another rhyme: oet.

i	long			short		
	vowel (+ending)	example	English	vowel (+ending)	example	English
	i	**zi**^{3} 志	*will*			
	iu	**ziu**^{3} 照	*shine*			
	im	**zim**^{3} 佔	*occupy by force*			
	in	**zin**^{3} 戰	*war*	**ing**	**zing**^{3} 正	*proper*
	ip	**zip**^{3} 接	*receive*	**ik**	**zik**^{1} 即	*now*
	it	**zit**^{3} 節	*festival*			

o	long			short		
	vowel (+ending)	example	English	vowel (+ending)	example	English
	o	**co**^{3} 錯	*wrong*	**ou**	**cou**^{3} 醋	*vinegar*
	oi	**oi**^{3} 愛	*love*			
	on	**hon**^{3} 看	*look*			
	ong	**tong**^{3} 燙	*scald*			
	ot	**hot**^{3} 渴	*thirsty*			
	ok	**gwok**^{3} 國	*country*			

u	long			short		
	vowel (+ending)	example	English	vowel (+ending)	example	English
	u	**fu**^{1} 夫	*husband*			
	ui	**fui**^{1} 灰	*grey*			
	un	**fun**^{1} 歡	*joy*	**ung**	**fung**^{1} 風	*wind*
	ut	**fut**^{3} 闊	*wide*	**uk**	**fuk**^{1} 福	*happiness*

yu	long			short		
	vowel (+ending)	example	English	vowel (+ending)	example	English
	yu	jyu^6 癒	*recover*			
	yun	jyun^6 願	*wish*			
	yut	jyut^6 月	*moon*			

3. Tones

Tones are expressed with numbers 1 to 6. There are three level tones (tone 1, tone 3 and tone 6), two rising tones (tone 2 and tone 5) and one falling tone (tone 4). Tone 4 is sometimes described as "super low level tone".

Table 3 Cantonese six tones *(Track 003)*

Tone	High Level	High Rising	Mid Level	Low Falling	Low Rising	Low Level
Description	high → 5	3 → 5	3 → 3	2 → 1	2 → 3	2 → 2
Pitch contour (5 / 4 / 3 / 2 / 1)	→	↗	→	↘	↗	→
Example 1	si^1 詩 *(poem)*	si^2 史 *(history)*	si^3 試 *(try)*	si^4 時 *(time)*	si^5 市 *(market)*	si^6 是 *(be)*
Example 2	jat^1 一 *(one)*	gau^2 九 *(nine)*	baat^3 八 *(eight)*	ling^4 零 *(zero)*	ng^5 五 *(five)*	ji^6 二 *(two)*
Example 3	saam^1 三 *(three)*	wun^2 碗 *(bowl)*	sai^3 細 *(small)*	ngau^4 牛 *(cow)*	naam^5 腩 *(belly)*	min^6 麵 *(noodle)*

Tone-embedded numerical sign

In order to make it easier to associate the numerals with the tone patterns, we have designed a tone-embedded numerical sign. Each tone number graphically tells you whether the tone is level, rising or falling, and also which level of pitch the tone belongs to. You will find this sign on top of every other page in each chapter of this book.

The differences between Jyutping (粵拼) and Yale (耶魯) system

In this section, we will focus on the differences between Jyutping and the Yale system so that those who have learned Cantonese in the Yale system can easily shift to Jyutping. These two systems are different, but the differences are not as major as one might think.

Initials: Only 3 out of 19 initials are differently spelt.

Finals: Only 6 out of 53 finals are differently spelt.

Tones: Numbers are used instead of diacritics.

The differences in Initials:

'J' and 'ch' in Yale are spelt 'z' and 'c' respectively in Jyutping. The sounds denoted by these two letters are similar to 'z' and 'c' in Hanyu Pinyin. 'Y' in Yale is a little tricky one, as it is spelt 'j' in Jyutping. 'J' is a symbol used in the International Phonetic Alphabet (IPA) as well as in some European languages such as German. Perhaps you can remember that shifting from "**Y**ale" to "**J**yutping" entails shifting from "y" to "j".

Yale	Jyutping
j	z
ch	c
y	j

The differences in Finals:

Basically the differences lie in how 'eu' in Yale is spelt in Jyutping. Basically it is spelt in two ways in Jyutping: 'oe' and 'eo'. 'Oe' and 'eo' are similar to 'her' in British English pronounced with rounded lips. 'Oe' is pronounced with the jaw placed lower than 'eo'. 'Eo' only occurs before the syllabic-final consonants 'i' , 'n' and 't'.

Yale	Jyutping
eu	oe
eung	oeng
euk	oek
eui	eoi
eun	eon
eut	eot

The differences in Tones:

They are the major differences between Yale and Jyutping. In Yale, tones are denoted by tone-marking diacritics and the use of 'h' in the spelling, whereas in Jyutping, numerals 1 – 6 are used to denote the six tones. Refer to the tone-embedded numeral sign in this book to remember which pitch pattern each number represents.

Yale	Jyutping
à / ā	a^1
á	a^2
a	a^3
àh	a^4
áh	a^5
ah	a^6

The pronunciation employed in this book

The pronunciation of each character in this book is based on the standard pronunciation of Hong Kong Cantonese, which may be found in the Linguistic Society of Hong Kong (LSHK) at: http://www.lshk.org/node/31.

As you become more familiar with Cantonese sounds and tones, you may find that sounds you hear in native Cantonese speakers' speech are often different from what you find in this textbook. This may be caused by the following factors:

1. Sound change is in progress in Cantonese.
2. Same words have alternative pronunciations.

Learners can improve their listening skills with the following guideline.

1. Initial "n-" is widely pronounced as "l-":

   e.g. nei^5 你 (*you*) ⟹ lei^5 , $naam^4$ 南 (*south*) ⟹ $laam^4$

2. Initial "ng-" and zero initial are interchangeable:

   e.g. ngo^5 我 (*I*) ⟹ o^5 , oi^3 愛 (*love*) ⟹ $ngoi^3$

3. Initial "gw- / kw-" before "o" are often pronounced as "g- / k-":

   e.g. $gwong^2$ 廣 (*wide*) ⟹ $gong^2$, $kwok^3$ 擴 (*broad*) ⟹ kok^3

4. Syllabic “ng” tends to become “m”:

   e.g. ng^5 五 (*five*) ⇒ m^5 , ng^4 吳 (Ng, surname) ⇒ m^4

5. Alternative initials are used:

   e.g. keoi^5 佢 (*he / she*) ⇒ heoi^5 , pou^2 • nei^2 普洱 (*Puer tea*) ⇒ pou^2 • lei^2 / bou^2 • lei^2

6. Final “-ng” is often pronounced as “-n”:

   e.g. hok^6 • saang^1 學生 (*student*) ⇒ hok^6 • saan^1 , pang^4 • jau^5 朋友 (*friend*) ⇒ pan^4 • jau^5

7. Final “-k” is often pronounced as “-t”:

   e.g. dak^6 • bit^6 特別 (*special*) ⇒ dat^6 • bit^6 , bak^1 北 (*north*) ⇒ bat^1

8. Final “-p” sometimes becomes “-t” (often found among Chinese northerners’ Cantonese):

   e.g. daap^3 • ce^1 搭車 (*commute*) ⇒ daat^3·ce^1 , sap^6 • jyut^6 十月 (*October*) ⇒ sat^6 • jyut^6

9. Final “-m” becomes “-n” (single phenomenon so far):

   e.g. dim^2 • gaai^2 點解 (*why*) ⇒ din^2 • gaai^2

10. Alternative finals are used:

    e.g. ni^1 呢 (*this*) ⇒ nei^1 / lei^1 , lai^4 嚟 (*come*) ⇒ lei^4 (employed sound in this book)

Useful Phrases

◇◇◇◇◇◇◇◇◇◇◇◇◇◇◇◇◇◇◇◇◇◇◇◇

The following are some of the essential phrases you come across when meeting Hong Kong people. They are short and easy to say. Let's practice and you will soon be getting by in Cantonese.

Hello! *(Track 004)*

Nei^5 hou^2! 你 好 ！ *Good day!* 你好！	Nei^5 hou^2! 你 好 ！ *Good day!* 你好！
Hou^2 • noi^6 • mou^5 • gin^3. 好 耐 冇 見 。 *Long time no see.* 很久没见。	Hou^2 • noi^6 • mou^5 • gin^3. 好 耐 冇 見 。 *Long time no see.* 很久没见。
Dim^2 aa^3? 點 呀 ？ *How's everything?* 怎样？	Ou^1 • kei^1 laa^1. O K 啦 。 *I'm fine.* 還好。
Mong^4 m^4 mong^4 aa^3? 忙 唔 忙 呀 ？ *Are you busy?* 忙不忙？	Hou^2 mong^4 aa^3. 好 忙 呀 。 *Very busy.* 很忙。

Good Morning! *(Track 005)*

Zou² • san⁴. 早 晨 。 *Good morning.* 早安。	Zou² • san⁴. 早 晨 。 *Good morning.* 早安。

Where are you going? *(Track 006)*

Heoi³ bin¹ • dou⁶ aa³ ? 去 邊 度 呀 ？ *Where are you going?* 去哪里？	Soeng⁵ • tong⁴. 上 堂 。 *Going to class.* 上课。

Have you eaten? (used as a greeting) *(Track 007)*

Sik⁶ • zo² • faan⁶ mei⁶ aa³ ? 食 咗 飯 未 呀 ？ *Have you eaten yet?* 吃过了吗？	Sik⁶ • zo² laa³. 食 咗 喇 。 *Yes, I have eaten.* 吃过了。	Mei⁶ sik⁶ aa³. 未 食 。 Not yet. 还没吃。

Thank you! *(Track 008)*

M^4 • goi^1 • saai^3 ! 唔 該 晒 ！ *Thank you (for the help / service)!* 谢谢。	M^4 • sai^2 m^4 • goi^1. 唔 駛 唔 該 。 *You're welcome.* 不用谢。
Do^1 • ze^6 ! 多 謝 ！ *Thank you (for the present / compliment)!* 谢谢。	M^4 • sai^2 do^1 • ze^6. 唔 駛 多 謝 。 *You're welcome.* 不用谢。

I cannot speak Cantonese. *(Track 009)*

	Ngo^5 m^4 sik^1 gong^2 Gwong^2 • dung^1 • waa^{2*}. 我 唔 識 講 廣 東 話 。 *I cannot speak Cantonese.* 我不会说广东话。

Do you speak English? *(Track 010)*

	Lei^5 sik^1 m^4 sik^4 gong^2 Jing^1 • man^{2*} aa^3 ? 你 識 唔 識 講 英 文 呀 ？ *Do you speak English?* 你会说英语吗？

Could you please translate for me? *(Track 011)*

	M^4 • goi^1 bong^1 ngo^5 faan^1 • jik^6. 唔 該 幫 我 翻 譯 。 *Please translate for me.* 请你帮我翻译。

†† The asterisk * indicates changed tones.

This one, please. *(Track 012)*

Ni1 go3 m4 • goi1 !
呢 個 唔 該 ！
This one, please.
麻烦你给我这个。

Numbers 1-10 *(Track 013)*

jat1	ji6	saam1	sei3	ng5	luk6	cat1	baat3	gau2	sap6
1	2	3	4	5	6	7	8	9	10

How much? *(Track 014)*

Gei2 • do1 cin2* aa3 ?
幾 多 錢 呀 ？
How much?
多少钱？

Money *(Track 015)*

jat1 man1	loeng5 man1	saam1 man1	sei3 man1	ng5 man1	luk6 man1	cat1 man1	baat3 man1	gau2 man1	sap6 man1
$1	$2	$3	$4	$5	$6	$7	$8	$9	$10

Where is the toilet? *(Track 016)*

Ci3 • so2 hai2 bin1 • dou6 aa3 ?
厠 所 喺 邊 度 呀 ？
Where is the toilet?
厕所在哪里？

Ni1 • dou6.
呢 度 。
Here.
这里。

Where is the MTR station? *(Track 017)*

Dei^6 • tit^3 • zaam^6 hai^2 bin^1 • dou^6 aa^3? 地 鐵 站 喺 邊 度 呀 ？ *Where is the MTR station?* 地铁站在哪里？	Go^2 • dou^6. 嗰 度 。 *Over there.* 那里。

Going home? *(Track 018)*

Faan^1 uk^1 • kei^2? 返 屋 企 ？ *Going home?* 回家？	Hai^6 aa^3. 係 呀 。 *Yes.* 是的。	M^4 hai^6 aa^3. 唔 係 呀 。 *No.* 不是。

Good-bye! *(Track 019)*

Zau^2 sin^1 laa^3. 走 先 啦 。 *I'm off now.* 先走啦。	Baai^1 • baai^3. 拜 拜 。 *Good-bye.* 再见。	Zoi^3 • gin^3. 再 見 。 *See you.* 再见。

1

Sik[1] san[1] pang[4] • jau[5]

識新朋友 *Making new friends*

Learning Tasks

- to show consideration
- to ask for directions (1)
- to ask whether one speaks Cantonese or not
- to ask for first and last names
- to ask for one's nationality
- to ask about a student's major

Grammar Notes

- verb '*to be*': hai[6] 係
- '*A-not-A*' questions: …m[4] 唔 …
- possession questions : jau[5] mou[5] 有冇
- adverb '*also / too / all*' : dou[1] 都
- '*where*' questions: bin[1] • dou[6] 邊度
- '*what*' questions: mat[1] • je[5] 乜嘢
- polite expressions

Sounds and Tones

- Difficult Cantonese initials

Supplementary Vocabulary

- nationalities
- languages
- major subjects
- common places to go

Exercise

- matching
- multiple choice
- fill in the blanks

1.1 Vocabulary *(Track 020)*

No.	Cantonese Romanization	Cantonese Characters	Putonghua & Chinese Characters	English
1.	m^{4} • hou^{2} • ji^{3} • si^{3}	唔好意思	duìbuqǐ 对不起	excuse me, sorry
2.	m^{4} • goi^{1}	唔該	xièxie 谢谢	thank you
3.	ceng^{2} • man^{6}	請問	qǐngwèn 请问	may I ask
4.	gwok^{3} • zai^{3} hok^{6} • saang^{1}	國際學生	guójì xuéshēng 国际学生	international student
5.	suk^{1} • se^{3}	宿舍	sùshè 宿舍	dormitory
6.	hai^{2}	喺	zài 在	be located at/in
7.	bin^{1} • dou^{6}	邊度	nǎli 哪里	where
8.	go^{2} • dou^{6}	嗰度	nàli 那里	there, over there
9.	ngo^{5}	我	wǒ 我	I, me
10.	nei^{5}	你	nǐ 你	you
11.	a) hai^{6}	係	shì 是	verb to be / yes
	b) m^{4} hai^{6}	唔係	búshì 不是	not / no
	c) hai^{6} m^{4} hai^{6}	係唔係	shì búshì 是不是	isn't it?
12.	sik^{1}	識	huì 会	can
13.	gong^{2}	講	shuō 说	speak
14.	Gwong^{2} • dung^{1} • waa^{2}*	廣東話	Guǎngdōng huà 广东话	the Cantonese language
15.	siu^{2} • siu^{2}	少少	yīdiǎn 一点	a little
16.	ngaam^{1} • ngaam^{1}	啱啱	gānggāng 刚刚	just
17.	lei^{4}	嚟	lái 来	come, arrive
18.	Hoeng^{1} • gong^{2}	香港	Xiānggǎng 香港	Hong Kong
19.	jau^{5}	有	yǒu 有	have / there is / there are
20.	mou^{5}	冇	méiyǒu 没有	do not have / there isn't / there aren't
21.	Zung^{1} • man^{4} meng^{2}*	中文名	Zhōngguó míngzi 中国名字	Chinese name
22.	giu^{3}	叫	jiào 叫	call
23.	me^{1}	咩	shénme 什么	what
24.	zyu^{2} • sau^{1}	主修	zhǔxiū 主修	major (in)
25.	gung^{1} • soeng^{1} gun^{2} • lei^{5}	工商管理	gōngshāng guǎnlǐ 工商管理	business administration
26.	ne^{1}	呢	ne 呢	how about
27.	dou^{1}	都	yě 也 / dōu 都	also / too

1.2 Tai-Lung's first day on campus. *(Track 021)*

M4 • hou2 • ji3 • si3, ceng2 • man6 gwok3 • zai3 hok6 • saang1 suk1 • se3 hai2 bin1 • dou6 aa3?
唔 好 意 思 ， 請 問 國 際 學 生 宿 舍 喺 邊 度 呀 ？
Excuse me, may I ask where the international students' dormitory is?
不好意思，请问国际学生宿舍在哪里？

Go2 • dou6.
嗰 度 。
Over there.
那里。

M4 • goi1.
唔 該 。
Thank you.
谢谢。

Waa4, nei5 sik1 gong2 Gwong2 • dung1 • waa2*?
嘩 ， 你 識 講 廣 東 話 ？
Wow, you can speak Cantonese?
哇，你会说广东话？

Sik1 siu2 • siu2.
識 少 少 。
Just a little.
会一点。

Nei5 hai6 bin1 • dou6 jan4 aa3?
你 係 邊 度 人 呀 ？
Where are you from?
你是哪里人？

Ngo5 hai6 Mei5 • gwok3 • jan4.
我 係 美 國 人 。
I'm American.
我是美国人。

Nei5 hai6 m4 hai6 ngaam1 • ngaam1 lei4 Hoeng1 • gong2 aa3?
你 係 唔 係 啱 啱 嚟 香 港 呀 ？
Did you just arrived in Hong Kong?
你是不是刚来香港？

Hai6 aa3.
係 呀 。
Yes.
对。

Nei5 jau5 mou5 Zung1 • man4 meng2* aa3?
你 有 冇 中 文 名 呀 ？
Do you have a Chinese name?
你有没有中国名字？

Jau5 aa3 , ngo5 giu3 Lei5 Daai6 • lung4. Nei5 giu3 me1 meng2* aa3?
有 呀 ， 我 叫 李 大 龍 。 你 叫 咩 名 呀 ？
Yes, my name is Lee Tai-Lung. What's your name?
有，我叫李大龙。你叫什么名字？

Ngo5 giu3 Can4 Gaa1 • man5.
我 叫 陳 嘉 敏 。
I'm Chan Ka-Man.
我叫陈嘉敏。

Nei5 zyu2 • sau1 me1 aa3?
你 主 修 咩 呀 ？
What do you major in?
你的专业是什么？

Ngo5 zyu2 • sau1 gung1 • soeng1 gun2 • lei5. Nei5 ne1?
我 主 修 工 商 管 理 。 你 呢 ？
I major in business administration. How about you?
我的专业是工商管理。你呢？

Ngo5 dou1 hai6 zyu2 • sau1 gung1 • soeng1 gun2 • lei5.
我 都 係 主 修 工 商 管 理 。
I major in business administration, too.
我也是主修工商管理。

1.3 Grammar Notes

1.3.1 Verb '*to be*' : hai6 係 *(Track 022)*

This verb is similar to the English verb to be (is/am/are/was/were).

P shì 是

Examples:

1. Ngo5 hai6 Gaa1 • naa4 • daai6 • jan4.
   我 係 加 拿 大 人 。
   I am Canadian.
   我是加拿大人。

2. Ngo^{5} hai^{6} hok^{6} • saang^{1}.
   我 係 學 生 。
   I am a student.
   我是学生。

1.3.2 '*A-not-A*' questions : … m^{4} 唔 … *(Track 023)*

This type of question is used when you expect someone to answer either yes or no. If yes, simply repeat the word 'A'. If no, say m^{4} 唔 + 'A'. 'Aa^{3}' is added as a tone-softener.

P A + bù 不 + A?

Examples:

1. *A:* Nei^{5} mong^{4} m^{4} mong^{4} aa^{3}?
   你 忙 唔 忙 呀 ？
   Are you busy?
   你忙不忙？

   B: Mong^{4} aa^{3}.
   忙 呀 。
   Yes.
   忙。

2. *A:* Nei^{5} hai^{6} m^{4} hai^{6} gaau^{1} • wun^{6} • sang^{1} aa^{3}?
   你 係 唔 係 交 換 生 呀 ？
   Are you an exchange student?
   你是不是交换学生？

   B: M^{4} hai^{6} aa^{3}.
   唔 係 呀 。
   No.
   不是。

1.3.3 Possession questions : jau^{5} mou^{5} 有冇 *(Track 024)*

This type of question is used to ask about possession. To reply, simply say "jau^{5} 有 (*yes*)", or "mou^{5} 冇 (*no*)".

P yǒu méiyǒu 有没有 …?

Examples:

1. *A:* Nei^{5} jau^{5} mou^{5} si^{4} • gaan^{3} aa^{3}?
   你 有 冇 時 間 呀 ？
   Do you have any time?
   你有没有时间呀？

   B: Jau^{5}.
   有 。
   Yes.
   有。

2. *A:* Nei^{5} jau^{5} mou^{5} cin^{2*} aa^{3}?
   你 有 冇 錢 呀 ？
   Do you have money?
   你有没有钱？

   B: Mou^{5}.
   冇 。
   No.
   没有。

1.3.4 Adverb '*also / too / all*' : dou[1] 都 (Track 025)

Used before a verb or adjective, dou[1] 都 means *also* or *all*.

P yě 也 / dōu 都

Examples:

1. Ngo[5] dou[1] heoi[3].
   我 都 去 。
   I will go, too.
   我也去。

2. Jan[4] • jan[4] dou[1] zi[1] • dou[3].
   人 人 都 知 道 。
   Everyone knows.
   每个人都知道。

1.3.5 '*Where*' questions : hai[2] bin[1] • dou[6] 喺邊度 (Track 026)

"Hai[2] bin[1] • dou[6] 喺邊度 (*Where*)" is used to ask about the location. To reply, you can point to the location and say "ni[1] • dou[6] 呢度 (*here*)", or "go[2] • dou[6] 嗰度 (*there*)".

P zài nǎli 在哪里

Examples:

1. *A:* Coffee Shop hai[2] bin[1] • dou[6] aa[3]?
   Coffee shop 喺 邊 度 呀 ？
   Where is the coffee shop?
   咖啡室在哪儿？

   B: Ni[1] • dou[6].
   呢 度 。
   Here.
   这里。

2. *A:* Keoi[5] • dei[6] hai[2] bin[1] • dou[6] aa[3]?
   佢 哋 喺 邊 度 呀 ？
   Where are they?
   他们在哪儿？

   B: Go[2] • dou[6].
   嗰 度 。
   There.
   那里。

†† In Hong Kong Cantonese, English terms such as *coffee shop*, are often used directly.

1.3.6 '*What*' questions : mat[1] • je[5] 乜嘢 (Track 027)

'What' question is expressed with "mat[1] • je[5] 乜嘢". Unlike English, "mat[1] • je[5] 乜嘢" does not move to the sentence-initial position. It has three variations:

me[1] • je[5] 咩嘢 , me[1] 咩 and mat[1] 乜.

P shénme 什么

Examples:

1. *A:* Nei^{5} soeng^{2} sik^{6} mat^{1} • je^{5} aa^{3}?
   你 想 食 乜 嘢 呀 ？
   What do you want to eat?
   你想吃什么？

   B: Sik^{6} syut^{3} • gou^{1}.
   食 雪 糕 。
   Eat ice cream.
   吃冰淇淋。

2. *A:* Nei^{5} jiu^{3} maai^{5} me^{1} aa^{3}?
   你 要 買 咩 呀 ？
   What do you want to buy?
   你要买什么？

   B: Maai^{5} saam^{1}.
   買 衫 。
   Buy clothes.
   买衣服。

1.3.7 Polite expressions : *(Track 028)*

C **m^{4} • hou^{2} • ji^{3} • si^{3} 唔好意思**
P duìbuqǐ 对不起 , láojià 劳驾
E excuse me / sorry *(apology / attracting attention)*

C **deoi^{3} • m^{4} • zyu^{6} 對唔住**
P duìbuqǐ 对不起 , bàoqiàn 抱歉
E sorry *(apology)*

C **m^{4} • gan^{2} • jiu^{3} 唔緊要**
P méi guānxi 没关系
E nevermind

C **m^{4} • goi^{1} 唔該**
P xièxie 谢谢 , láojià 劳驾 , máfan nǐ 麻烦你
E thank you *(for help / services rendered)*
excuse me *(attracting attention)*

C **do^{1} • ze^{6} 多謝**
P xièxie 谢谢
E thank you *(for compliments / gifts / treats)*

C **m^{4} • sai^{2} haak^{3} • hei^{3} 唔駛客氣**
P bú yòng kèqi 不用客气
E you're welcome

Examples:

1. M^{4} • hou^{2} • ji^{3} • si^{3}, ngo^{5} ci^{4} • dou^{3}.
   唔 好 意 思 ， 我 遲 到 。
   Sorry, I am late.
   唔好意思，我迟到。

2. Deoi^{3} • m^{4} • zyu^{6}, bong^{1} • m^{4} • dou^{2} nei^{5}.
   對 唔 住 ， 幫 唔 到 你 。
   I'm sorry, I can't help you.
   对不起，帮不上忙。

3. M[4] • goi[1], maai[4] • daan[1].
   唔 該 ， 埋 單 。
   Excuse me. Bill, please!
   麻煩你，結帳。

4. Do[1] • ze[6] nei[5] ceng[2] sik[6] • faan[6].
   多 謝 你 請 食 飯 。
   Thank you for dinner.
   謝謝你請客。

1.4 Difficult Cantonese initials

In this section, you will focus on some of the initial sounds that English and Putonghua speakers often find difficult to pronounce.

Listen carefully and mimic the following words.

(a) **ng** : similar to 'ng' in 'singer'in English. *(Track 029)*

1.	ngo[6]	餓	hungry	3. ngau[4]	牛	cow
2.	ngaang[6]	硬	solid	4. ngok[6]	樂	music

(b) **c** : similar to 'ch' in 'China' in English (without rounded lips). *(Track 030)*

1.	caa[4]	茶	tea	3. cin[2]*	錢	money
2.	ce[1]	車	car	4. cou[4]	嘈	noisy

(c) **h** : similar to 'h' in 'how' in English. *(Track 031)*

1.	haam[4]	鹹	salty	3. hok[6]	學	learn
2.	heoi[3]	去	go	4. hou[2]	好	good

(d) **gw** : similar to the initial 'g' + 'u' in Putonghua. *(Track 032)*

1.	gwaa[1]	瓜	melon	3. gwo[2]	果	fruit
2.	gwaan[3]	慣	accustomed	4. gwat[1]	骨	bone

(e) **kw** : similar to the initial 'k' + 'u' in Putonghua. *(Track 033)*

1.	kwaa[1]	誇	exaggerate	3. kwaang[3]	逛	wander
2.	kwan[4]	裙	skirt	4. kwong[4]	狂	mad

†† Young people tend to pronounce 'n-' as ' l-', and drop 'ng-' and pronounce it as 'zero' initial.

1.5 Supplementary Vocabulary

1.5.1 Nationality *(Track 034)*

No.	Cantonese Romanization	Chinese	Putonghua & Chinese Characters	English
1.	Mei^5 • gwok^3 • jan^4	美國人	Měiguórén 美国人	American
2.	Ou^3 • zau^1 • jan^4	澳洲人	Àodàlìyàrén 澳大利亚人	Australian
3.	Jing^1 • gwok^3 • jan^4	英國人	Yīngguórén 英国人	British
4.	Gaa^1 • naa^4 • daai^6 • jan^4	加拿大人	Jiānádàrén 加拿大人	Canadian
5.	Zung^1 • gwok^3 • jan^4	中國人	Zhōngguórén 中国人	Chinese
6.	Fei^1 • leot^6 • ban^1 • jan^4	菲律賓人	Fēilǜbīnrén 菲律宾人	Filipino
7.	Faat^3 • gwok^3 • jan^4	法國人	Fǎguórén 法国人	French
8.	Jan^3 • dou^6 • jan^4	印度人	Yìndùrén 印度人	Indian
9.	Jat^6 • bun^2 • jan^4	日本人	Rìběnrén 日本人	Japanese
10.	Hon^4 • gwok^3 • jan^4	韓國人	Hánguórén 韩国人	Korean

1.5.2 Languages *(Track 035)*

No.	Cantonese Romanization	Chinese	Putonghua & Chinese Characters	English
1.	Gwong^2• dung^1• waa^{2}*	廣東話	Guǎngzhōuhuà 广州话	Cantonese
2.	Jing^1• man^{2}*	英文	Yīngyǔ 英语	English
3.	Faat^3• man^{2}*	法文	Fǎyǔ 法语	French
4.	Ji^3• daai^6• lei^6• waa^{2}*	意大利話	Yìdàlìyǔ 意大利语	Italian
5.	Jat^6• man^{2}*	日文	Rìyǔ 日语	Japanese
6.	Pou^2• tung^1• waa^{2}*	普通話	Pǔtōnghuà 普通话	Putonghua
7.	Sai^1• baan^1• ngaa^4• waa^{2}*	西班牙話	Xībānyáyǔ 西班牙语	Spanish
8.	Fei^1• leot^6• ban^1• waa^{2}*	菲律賓話	Fēilǜbīnyǔ 菲律宾语	Tagalog
9.	Taai^3• man^{2}*	泰文	Tàiyǔ 泰语	Thai
10.	Baa^1• gei^1• si^1• taan^2• waa^{2}*	巴基斯坦話	Bājīsītǎnyǔ 巴基斯坦语	Urdu

 1.5.3 Major subjects *(Track 036)*

No.	Cantonese Romanization	Chinese	Putonghua & Chinese Characters	English
1.	gin^{3} • zuk^{1}	建築	jiànzhù 建筑	architecture
2.	man^{4} • hok^{6}	文學	wénxué 文学	arts
3.	gung^{1} • soeng^{1} gun^{2} • lei^{5}	工商管理	gōngshāng guǎnlǐ 工商管理	business administration
4.	gaau^{3} • juk^{6}	教育	jiàoyù 教育	education
5.	gung^{1} • cing^{4}	工程	gōngchéng 工程	engineering
6.	jan^{4} • man^{4} • hok^{6}	人文學	rénwénxué 人文学	humanities
7.	faat^{3} • leot^{6}	法律	fǎlǜ 法律	law
8.	ji^{1} • hok^{6}	醫學	yīxué 医学	medicine
9.	fo^{1} • hok^{6}	科學	kēxué 科学	science
10.	se^{5} • wui^{2*} fo^{1} • hok^{6}	社會科學	shèhuì kēxué 社会科学	social science

1.5.4 Common places to go *(Track 037)*

No.	Cantonese Romanization	Chinese	Putonghua & Chinese Characters	English
1.	ting^{4} • ce^{1} • coeng^{4}	停車場	tíngchēchǎng 停车场	car park
2.	zau^{2} • lau^{4}	酒樓	fànguǎn 饭馆	Chinese restaurant
3.	hei^{3} • jyun^{2}	戲院	diànyǐngyuàn 电影院	cinema
4.	zau^{2} • dim^{3}	酒店	jiǔdiàn 酒店	hotel
5.	maa^{5} • tau^{4}	碼頭	mǎtóu 码头	pier
6.	ging^{2} • caat^{3} • guk^{2*}/ caai^{1} • gun^{2}	警察局 / 差館	gōng'ānjú 公安局	police station
7.	jau^{4} • guk^{2*}	郵局	yóujú 邮局	post office
8.	soeng^{1} • coeng^{4}	商場	shāngchǎng 商场	shopping center
9.	ciu^{1} •(kap^{1})• si^{5} •(coeng^{4})	超級市場	chāojí shìchǎng 超级市场	supermarket
10.	dik^{1} • si^{2*} • zaam^{6}	的士站	chūzūchē zhàn 出租车站	taxi stand

1.6 Exercise

1.6.1 Matching

1. ____ m^{4} • goi^{1} 唔該 — A. sorry
2. ____ m^{4} • hou^{2} • ji^{3} • si^{3*} 唔好意思 — B. thank you *(for gifts)*
3. ____ deoi^{3} • m^{4} • zyu^{6} 對唔住 — C. thank you *(for a service)*
4. ____ do^{1} • ze^{6} 多謝 — D. nevermind
5. ____ m^{4} • gan^{2} • jiu^{3} 唔緊要 — E. sorry *(formal apology)*

1.6.2 Multiple choice

1. *What is your name?*
   Nei^{5} 你 giu^{3} 叫 ____________ meng^{2*} 名 aa^{3} 呀？

   A. hai^{2} bin^{1} • dou^{6} 喺邊度　　B. me^{1} 咩　　C. jau^{5} mou^{5} 有冇

2. *Do you have money?*
   Nei^{5} 你 ____________ cin^{2*} 錢 aa^{3} 呀？

   A. jau^{5} m^{4} jau^{5} 有唔有　　B. mou^{5} jau^{5} 冇有　　C. jau^{5} mou^{5} 有冇

3. *Do you speak Cantonese?*
   Nei^{5} 你 sik^{1} 識 ____________ sik^{1} 識 gong^{2} 講 Gwong^{2} • dung^{1} • waa^{2*} 廣東話 aa^{3} 呀？

   A. hai^{6} 係　　B. me^{1} 咩　　C. m^{4} 唔

4. *Me, too.*
   Ngo^{5} 我 ____________ hai^{6} 係。

   A. dou^{1} 都　　B. me^{1} 咩　　C. m^{4} 唔

5. *Where is Pizza Hut?*
   Pizza Hut ____________ aa^{3} 呀？

   A. hai^{2} bin^{1} • dou^{6} 喺邊度　　B. me^{1} 咩　　C. jau^{5} mou^{5} 有冇

1.6.3 Fill in the blanks

				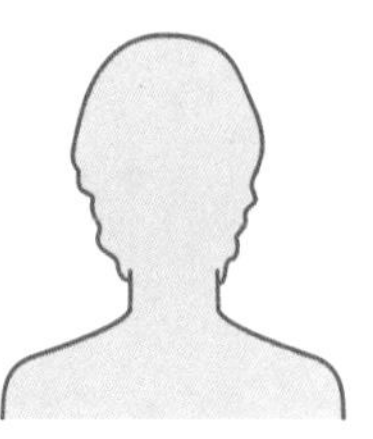
Peter	***Mary***	***Jane***	***Paul***	**YOU**
Canadian 加拿大人	American 美國人	Filipina 菲律賓人	Chinese 中國人	
speak French 講法文	speak English 講英文	speak Tagalog 講菲律賓話	speak Putonghua 講普通話	

1. ***Peter*** hai^6 __________________ jan^4, sik^1 gong^2 __________________ .

2. ***Mary*** hai^6 __________________ jan^4, sik^1 gong^2 __________________ .

3. ***Jane*** hai^6 __________________ jan^4, sik^1 gong^2 __________________ .

4. ***Paul*** hai^6 __________________ jan^4, sik^1 gong^2 __________________ .

5. **Ngo^5** hai^6 __________________ jan^4, sik^1 gong^2 __________________ .

2

Hai^2 faan^6 • tong^4 sik^6 aan^3

喺飯堂食晏 *Lunch in the canteen*

Learning Tasks

- to start a conversation
- to introduce each other
- to indicate your preferred name
- to talk about a duration of time
- to ask how long one has been living somewhere
- to ask where one lives
- to order food and drinks

Grammar Notes

- personal plural suffix: dei^6 哋
- '*to* / *for*' + person: bei^2 俾
- possessive: ge^3 嘅
- terms of address
- completion marker: zo^2 咗
- '*how long*' questions: gei^2 • noi^6 幾耐
- years & months: nin^4 年 , jyut^6 月
- negation: m^4 唔 , mou^5 冇 , mei^6 未

Sounds and Tones

- Difficlut Cantonese final endings

Supplementary Vocabulary

- months of the year
- Chinese surnames
- fast food
- drinks

Exercise

- matching
- multiple choice
- fill in the blanks

2.1 Vocabulary *(Track 038)*

No.	Cantonese Romanization	Cantonese Characters	Putonghua & Chinese Characters	English
1.	a) zo^{2}	咗	le 了	completion marker
	b) sik^{6} • zo^{2} • faan^{6}	食咗飯	chīle fàn 吃了饭	have eaten (a meal)
	c) sik^{6} • zo^{2} • faan^{6} mei^{6} aa^{3}	食咗飯未呀	chīle fàn méiyǒu 吃了饭没有	have you eaten yet?
2.	zung^{6} mei^{6} sik^{6}	仲未食	hái méi chī 还没吃	have not eaten yet
3.	jat^{1} • cai^{4} sik^{6} laa^{1}	一齊食啦	yìqǐ chī ba 一起吃吧	let's eat together
4.	a) hou^{2}	好	hǎo 好 / hěn 很	yes / very
	b) hou^{2} aa^{3}	好呀	hǎo a 好啊	sure
	c) hou^{2} hoi^{1} • sam^{1}	好開心	hěn gāoxìng 很高兴	very happy
5.	gaai^{3} • siu^{6}…bei^{2} nei^{5} sik^{1}	介紹…俾你識	gěi nǐ jièshào 给你介绍 …	introduce …to you
6.	ge^{3}	嘅	de 的	possessive marker
7.	tung^{4} • hok^{6}	同學	tóngxué 同学	classmate
8.	keoi^{5}	佢	tā 他 / 她 / 它	he/she/it
9.	a) dei^{6}	哋	men 们	plural suffix
	b) ngo^{5} • dei^{6}	我哋	wǒmen 我们	we, us
	c) nei^{5} • dei^{6}	你哋	nǐmen 你们	you (plural)
	d) keoi^{5} • dei^{6}	佢哋	tāmen 他 / 她 / 它们	they, them
10.	sin^{1} • saang^{1}	先生	xiānsheng 先生	Mr., Sir
11.	siu^{2} • ze^{2}	小姐	xiǎojie 小姐	Miss
12.	sik^{1} • dou^{2}	識到	kěyǐ rènshi 可以认识	get acquainted
13.	a) gei^{2} • noi^{6}	幾耐	lái le duōjiǔ 多久	how long (duration)
	b) lei^{4} • zo^{2} gei^{2} • noi^{6}	嚟咗幾耐	duōjiǔ 来了多久	how long have you been here?
14.	jat^{1} nin^{4}	一年	yī nián 一年	one year
15.	saam^{1} go^{3} jyut^{6}	三個月	sān ge yuè 三个月	three months
16.	zyu^{6} hai^{2} bin^{1} • dou^{6}	住喺邊度	zhù zài nǎli 住在哪里	where do you live?
17.	zyu^{6} hai^{2} suk^{1} • se^{3}	住喺宿舍	zhù zài sùshè 住在宿舍	live in dormitory
18.	a) sik^{6} me^{1}	食咩	chī shénme 吃什么	what will you eat?
	b) sik^{6} ji^{3} • fan^{2}	食意粉	chī yìdàlì miàn 吃意大利面	eat pasta
19.	jam^{2} gaa^{3} • fe^{1}	飲咖啡	hē kāfēi 喝咖啡	drink coffee
20.	me^{1} • lei^{4} • gaa^{3}	咩嚟㗎	shì shénme 是什么	what is it?

21.	jit^6 jyun^1 • joeng^1 / jin^1 • joeng^1	熱鴛鴦	rè yuānyang 热鸳鸯	hot coffee mixed with milk tea (a unique Hong Kong-style drink)
22.	gaa^1	加	jiā 加	add
23.	naai^5 • caa^4	奶茶	nǎichá 奶茶	tea with milk
24.	dung^3 ning^{2*} • caa^4	凍檸茶	bīng níngméng chá 冰柠檬茶	cold lemon tea

2.2 Ka-Man and Tai-Lung meet two friends in the canteen. They queue up to order lunch. *(Track 039)*

Sik^6 • zo^2 • faan^6 mei^6 aa^3?
食 咗 飯 未 呀 ？
Have you eaten yet?
吃了饭没有？

Zung^6 mei^6 sik^6, jat^1 • cai^4 sik^6 laa^1.
仲 未 食 ， 一 齊 食 啦 。
Not yet. Let's eat together.
还没吃，一起吃吧。

Hou^2 aa^3. Ngo^5 gaai^3 • siu^6 ngo^5 ge^3 tung^4 • hok^6 bei^2 nei^5 • dei^6 sik^1. Keoi^5 hai^6 Lei^5 Daai^6 • lung^4, keoi^5 • dei^6 hai^6 Maa^5 Wing^6 • si^1, Wong^4 Gaa^1 • naam^4.
好 呀 。 我 介 紹 我 嘅 同 學 俾 你 哋 識 ： 佢 係 李 大 龍 、 佢 哋 係 馬 詠 詩 、 黃 家 男 。
Sure. Let me introduce my classmates. He's Lee Tai-Lung. They're Ma Wing-Sze and Wong Ka-Nam.
我把我的同学们介绍给你们：他是李大龙，他们是马咏诗，黄家男。

Maa^5 siu^2 • ze^2, Wong^4 sin^1 • saang^1, hou^2 hoi^1 • sam^1 sik^1 • dou^2 nei^5 • dei^6.
馬 小 姐 、 黃 先 生 ， 好 開 心 識 到 你 哋 。
Miss Ma, Mr. Wong, nice to meet you both.
马小姐、黄先生，很高兴认识你们。

Giu^3 ngo^5 Gaa^1 • naam^4 laa^1!
叫 我 家 男 啦 ！
Just call me Ka-Nam.
叫我家男吧！

Gaa^1 • naam^4, nei^5 • dei^6 lei^4 • zo^2 Hoeng^1 • gong^2 gei^2 • noi^6 aa^3?
家 男 ， 你 哋 嚟 咗 香 港 幾 耐 呀 ？
Ka-Nam, how long have you been in Hong Kong?
家男，你们来香港多久了？

Ngo^5 lei^4 • zo^2 jat^1 nin^4.
我 嚟 咗 一 年 。
I've been here for a year.
我来了一年。

Ngo^5 lei^4 • zo^2 saam^1 go^3 jyut^6.
我 嚟 咗 三 個 月 。
I've been here for three months.
我来了三个月。

Nei^5 • dei^6 zyu^6 hai^2 bin^1 • dou^6 aa^3?
你 哋 住 喺 邊 度 呀 ？
Where do you live?
你们住在哪里？

Ngo^5 • dei^6 dou^1 zyu^6 hai^2 suk^1 • se^3.
我 哋 都 住 喺 宿 舍 。
We all live in the dormitory.
我们都住在宿舍。

It's Ka-Man's turn to order.

Sik^6 me^1 aa^3.
食 咩 呀 ？
What would you like to eat?
吃什么？

Faan^1 • ke^2 ngau^4 • juk^6 faan^6, dung^3 jyun^1 • joeng^1, m^4 • goi^1.
番 茄 牛 肉 飯 ， 凍 鴛 鴦 ， 唔 該 。
Beef & tomato with rice, cold 'mandarin duck', please.
要番茄牛肉饭，冻鸳鸯吧。

Jyun^1 • joeng^1 hai^6 me^1 • lei^4 • gaa^3?
「鴛 鴦」 係 咩 嚟 㗎 ？
What's 'mandarin duck'?
「鸳鸯」是什么？

Jyun^1 • joeng^1 hai^6 gaa^3 • fe^1 gaa^1 naai^5 • caa^4.
「鴛 鴦」 係 咖 啡 加 奶 茶 。
'Mandarin duck' is coffee mixed with t milk tea.
「鸳鸯」是咖啡加奶茶。

Haa^6 jat^1 wai^{2*}, m^4 • goi^1!
下 一 位 ， 唔 該 ！
Next please!
下 一 位 ！

Juk^6 • zoeng^3 ji^3 • fan^2.
肉 醬 意 粉 。
Spaghetti bolognese.
肉 酱 意 粉 。

Jam^2 me^1 aa^3?
飲 咩 呀 ？
What would you like to drink?
喝 什 么 ？

Dung^3 ning^{2*} • caa^4, m^4 • goi^1.
凍 檸 茶 ， 唔 該 。
Cold tea with lemon, please.
请 给 我 冰 柠 檬 茶 。

2.3 Grammar Notes

2.3.1 Personal plural suffix : dei^6 哋 *(Track 040)*

"Dei^6 哋 " is a personal plural marker. It is similar to men 們 in Putonghua, but its use is usually limited to personal pronouns. It can also be suffixed to "jan^4 人 " to form a term for *people*.

men 們

C	E
ngo^5 • dei^6 我哋	we
nei^5 • dei^6 你哋	you (plural)
keoi^5 • dei^6 佢哋	they
jan^4 • dei^6 人哋	people

Examples:

1. Ngo^5 • dei^6 hai^6 daai^6 • hok^6 • saang^1.
   我 哋 係 大 學 生 。
   We are university students.
   我 们 是 大 学 生 。

2. *A:* Nei^{5}• dei^{6} soeng^{2} maai^{5} me^{1} aa^{3}?
你 哋 想 買 咩 呀 ?
What do you guys want to buy?
你们想买什么?

B: Ti^{1}• seot^{1}.
T 恤 。
T-shirt.
T 恤 衫 。

2.3.2 Preposition *'to / for'* : bei^{2} 俾 *(Track 041)*

Like gěi 给 in Putonghua, "bei^{2} 俾" marks the person for whom the action concerned is performed. In English, it is often expressed by *to* or *for*. When introducing a friend to someone, the following pattern is used: "gaai^{3} • siu^{6} 介紹 (*introduce*) + a friend + bei^{2} 俾 (*to*) + someone + sik^{1} 識 (*recognize*)"

P gěi 给

Examples:

1. Ngo^{5} gaai^{3} • siu^{6} ngo^{5} tung^{4} • fong^{2} bei^{2} nei^{5} sik^{1}.
我 介 紹 我 同 房 俾 你 識 。
Let me introduce my roommate to you.
我把室友介绍给你。

2. Nei^{5} gaai^{3} • siu^{6} jat^{1} go^{3} Hoeng^{1} • gong^{2} • jan^{4} bei^{2} ngo^{5} sik^{1} aa^{1}!
你 介 紹 一 個 香 港 人 俾 我 識 吖 !
Please introduce a Hong Kong person to me!
你介绍一个香港人给我认识吧!

2.3.3 Possessive : ge^{3} 嘅 *(Track 042)*

"Ge^{3} 嘅" corresponds to de 的 in Putonghua. It is often used before a noun to form a possessive construction, e.g. "ngo^{5} ge^{3} syu^{1} 我嘅書 (*my book*)".

P de 的

Examples:

1. Keoi^{5} hai^{6} ngo^{5} ge^{3} hou^{2} pang^{4} • jau^{5}.
佢 係 我 嘅 好 朋 友 。
He is a good friend of mine.
他是我的好朋友。

2. Faan^{6} • tong^{4} ge^{3} je^{5} m^{4} hou^{2} • sik^{6}.
飯 堂 嘅 嘢 唔 好 食 。
Food from the canteen is not delicious.
食堂的东西不好吃。

2.3.4 Cantonese term of address : *(Track 043)*

Cantonese terms of address come after a propr noun, e.g. "Can4 sin1 • saang1 陳先生 (*Mr. Chan*)". In daily conversation, "sin1 • saang1 先生 (*Mr.*)" and "taai3• taai2* 太太 (*Mrs.*)" will be shortened to "saang1 生" and "taai2* 太" respectively, e.g. "Lei5 saang1 李生 (*Mr. Lee*)", "Lei5 taai2* 李太 (*Mrs. Lee*)".

Common address terms in Cantonese:

C	P	E
sin1 • saang1 先生	xiānshēng 先生 / lǎoshī 老师	Mr. / teacher
taai3 • taai2* 太太	tàitài 太太	Mrs. Madam
siu2 • ze2 小姐	xiǎojie 小姐 （没有贬义）	Miss

Examples:

1. Lei5 saang1, Lei5 taai2*, zou2 • san4.
   李 生 、 李 太 ， 早 晨 。
   Mr. and Mrs. Lee, good morning!
   李先生、李太太，早安。

2. *A:* Miss Zau1 , heoi3 bin1 • dou6 aa3 ?
   Miss 周 ， 去 邊 度 呀 ？
   Miss Chow, where are you going?
   周小姐，上哪儿去呀？

   B: Jau4 • seoi2.
   游 水 。
   I'm going to swim.
   游泳 。

2.3.5 Completion marker : zo2 咗 *(Track 044)*

"Zo2 咗" is placed right after a verb to denote the completion of action.

P le 了

Examples:

1. *A:* Nei5 tai2 • zo2 me1 hei3 aa3?
   你 睇 咗 咩 戲 呀 ？
   What movie did you see?
   你看了什么电影？

   B: Haa1• lei6 Bo1• dak6 .
   哈 利 波 特 。
   Harry Potter.
   哈利波特 。

2. Ngo5 maai5 • zo2 jat1 bun2 syu1.
   我 買 咗 一 本 書 。
   I bought a book.
   我买了一本书。

2.3.6 '*How long*' questions : gei2 noi6 幾耐 *(Track 045)*

"Gei2 • noi6 / gei2 • loi6 幾耐" is used to ask about the time duration. It is often placed at the sentence final position, followed by the sentence particle "aa3 呀".

P duō jiǔ 多久

Examples:

1. *A:* Nei5 zyu6 hai2 Hoeng1 • gong2 gei2 • noi6 aa3?
   你 住 係 香 港 幾 耐 呀 ？
   How long have you lived in Hong Kong?
   你在香港住了多久了？

   B: Saam1 nin4.
   三 年 。
   Three years.
   三年 。

2. *A:* Nei5 hok6 • zo2 Gwong2 • dung1 • waa2* gei2 • noi6 aa3?
   你 學 咗 廣 東 話 幾 耐 呀 ？
   How long have you been learning Cantonese?
   你学广东话学了多久了？

   B: Jat1 nin4.
   一 年 。
   One year.
   一年 。

2.3.7 Talking about years and months : nin4 年 & jyut6 月 *(Track 046)*

The number of years is expressed with a number followed by "nin4 / lin4 年 (*year*)". In case of the number of months, the classifier "go3 個" is placed between a number and "jyut6 月 (*month*)".

Examples:

1. Ngo5 zyu6 hai2 Hoeng1 • gong2 bun3 nin4.
   我 住 係 香 港 半 年 。
   I've lived in Hong Kong for half a year.
   我在香港住了半年了。

2. Ngo5 hok6 • zo2 Gwong2 • dung1 • waa2* leong5 go3 jyut6 laa3.
   我 學 咗 廣 東 話 兩 個 月 啦 。
   I've been learning Cantonese for two months.
   我学广东话学了两个月了。

2.3.8 Negation : m4 唔，mou5 冇，mei6 未 *(Track 047)*

Cantonese negation words typically start with the initial m, all of which are used before a verb or adjective construction. Each word denotes different types of negation as in the following chart. For negative imperatives, use "m4 • hou2 唔好" (see Lesson 8).

C	P	E
m⁴ 唔	bù 不	negation of state, one's will, habitual action, etc.
mou⁵ 冇	méiyou 没有	negation of ownership (unrealized action)
mei⁶ 未	hái méi 还没	negation of anticipated action

Examples:

1. Ngo⁵ hou² baau². M⁴ soeng² sik⁶.
   我 好 飽 。 唔 想 食 。
   I am full. I don't want to eat.
   我很饱。不想吃。

2. Ngo⁵ mou⁵ sik⁶.
   我 冇 食 。
   I didn't eat it.
   我没有吃。

3. Ngo⁵ zung⁶ mei⁶ sik⁶.
   我 仲 未 食 。
   I haven't eaten yet.
   我还没吃。

2.4 Difficult Cantonese final endings

There are six kinds of Cantonese syllables that end with consonants: '-m', '-n', '-ng', '-p', '-t', and '-k'. In this section, we will focus on those with '-m', '-p', '-t', and '-k' endings, which learners often find difficult to pronounce properly.

Listen carefully and mimic the following words.

(a) **-m** : similar to 'm' in 'jumping' in English (lips kept closed for 'm'). *(Track 048)*

1.	dim² • sam¹	點心	dim sum	3.	sam¹ • lam⁴	森林	forest
2.	saam¹ dim²	三點	three o'clock	4.	gaam³ • laam²*	橄欖	olive

(b) **-p** : similar to 'yep' in English (air kept unreleased for 'p'). *(Track 049)*

1.	laap⁶• saap³	垃圾	rubbish	3.	daap³ • lip¹	搭𨋢	take a lift
2.	zaap⁶ • hap⁶	集合	gather	4.	sap⁶ jip⁶	十頁	ten pages

(c) -t : similar to 'hotdog'in English (air kept unreleased for 't'). *(Track 050)*

1.	cat^{1} • jyut^{6}	七月	July	3.	faat^{3} • leot^{6}	法律	law
2.	zit^{3} • jat^{6}	節日	festival	4.	gaat^{6} • zaat^{2*}	曱甴	cockroach

(d) -k : similar to 'k' in 'cocktail' in English (air kept unreleased for 'k'). *(Track 051)*

1.	baak^{6} • sik^{1}	白色	white	3.	sik^{6} • joek^{6}	食藥	take medicine
2.	zik^{6} • mok^{6}	寂寞	lonely	4.	muk^{6} • dik^{1}	目的	purpose

2.5 Supplementary Vocabulary

2.5.1 Month of the year *(Track 052)*

No.	Cantonese Romanization	Chinese	Putonghua Romanization	English
1.	jat^{1} • jyut^{6}	一月	yī yuè 一月	January
2.	ji^{6} • jyut^{6}	二月	èr yuè 二月	February
3.	saam^{1} • jyut^{6}	三月	sān yuè 三月	March
4.	sei^{3} • jyut^{6}	四月	sì yuè 四月	April
5.	ng^{5} • jyut^{6}	五月	wǔ yuè 五月	May
6.	luk^{6} • jyut^{6}	六月	liù yuè 六月	June
7.	cat^{1}• jyut^{6}	七月	qī yuè 七月	July
8.	baat^{3} • jyut^{6}	八月	bā yuè 八月	August
9.	gau^{2} • jyut^{6}	九月	jiǔ yuè 九月	September
10.	sap^{6} • jyut^{6}	十月	shí yuè 十月	October
11.	sap^{6} • jat^{1} • jyut^{6}	十一月	shíyī yuè 十一月	November
12.	sap^{6} • ji^{6} • jyut^{6}	十二月	shí'èr yuè 十二月	December

2.5.2 Chinese surnames *(Track 053)*

No.	Cantonese Romanization	Chinese	Putonghua Romanization	Common spellings used in Hong Kong
1.	Can^{4}	陳	Chén 陈	Chan
2.	Zau^{1}	周	Zhōu 周	Chow, Chau
3.	Zoeng^{1}	張	Zhāng 张	Cheung

4.	Ho^4	何	Hé 何	Ho
5.	Lam^4	林	Lín 林	Lam
6.	Lau^4	劉	Liú 刘	Lau
7.	Lei^5	李	Lǐ 李	Lee, Li
8.	Loeng^4	梁	Liáng 梁	Leung
9.	Ng^4	吳	Wú 吴	Ng
10.	Wong^4	王	Wáng 王	Wong

2.5.3 Fast food *(Track 054)*

No.	Cantonese Romanization	Chinese	Putonghua Romanization	English
1.	caa^1 • siu^1 faan^6	叉燒飯	chāshāo fàn 叉烧饭	BBQ pork on rice
2.	Joeng^4 • zau^1 caau^2 • faan^6	楊州炒飯	yángzhōu chǎofàn 扬州炒饭	Yangzhou-style fried rice
3.	gon^1 • caau^2 ngau^4 • ho^2*	乾炒牛河	gānchǎo niúhé 干炒牛河	fried rice noodles with beef
4.	hon^3 • bou^2 baau^1	漢堡飽	hànbǎobāo 汉堡包	hamburger
5.	zyu^1 • paa^2* faan^6	豬扒飯	zhūpái fàn 猪排饭	pork chop on rice
6.	syu^4 • tiu^2*	薯條	shǔtiáo 薯条	French fries
7.	saa^1 • leot^2*	沙律	shālā 沙拉	salad
8.	saam^1 • man^4 • zi^6	三文治	sānmíngzhì 三明治	sandwich
9.	ji^3 • fan^2	意粉	yìdàlìmiàn 意大利面	spaghetti
10.	loeng^5 • sung^3 • faan^6	兩餸飯	liǎng cài tàocān 两菜套餐	two dishes with rice

2.5.4 Drinks *(Track 055)*

No.	Cantonese Romanization	Chinese	Putonghua Romanization	English
1.	be^1 • zau^2	啤酒	píjiǔ 啤酒	beer
2.	zyu^1 • gu^1* • lik^1*	朱古力	qiǎokèlì 巧克力	chocolate (milk)
3.	guk^1 • faa^1 • caa^4	菊花茶	júhuāchá 菊花茶	chrysanthemum tea
4.	ho^2 • lok^6	可樂	kělè 可乐	coke

5.	caa4	茶	chá 茶	tea
6.	hou2 • laap6 • hak1	好立克	hǎolìkè 好立克	Horlicks melted milk
7.	caang2 • zap1	橙汁	chéngzhī 橙汁	orange juice
8.	cat1 • hei2	七喜	qīxǐ 七喜	7 Up
9.	seoi2	水	shuǐ 水	water
10.	ning2* • mat6	檸蜜	níngmì 柠蜜	lemon water with honey

†† To specify a hot or cold drink, simply add "jit6 熱" or "dung3 凍" in front of the names of drinks.

2.6 Exercise

2.6.1 Matching

1. keoi5 • dei6 佢哋 ______ A. my
2. ngo5 ge3 我嘅 ______ B. can speak
3. hoi1 • sam1 開心 ______ C. Mrs. Wong
4. Wong4 taai2* 王太 ______ D. happy
5. sik1 gong2 識講 ______ E. they

2.6.2 Multiple choice

1. *Let me introduce her to you.*

   Ngo5 我 gaai3 • siu6 介紹 keoi5 佢 ______ nei5 你 sik1 識。

   A. gei2 幾　　B. zo2 咗　　C. bei2 俾

2. *How long you have been learning Cantonese?*

   Nei5 你 hok6 • zo2 學咗 Gwong2 • dung1 • waa2* 廣東話 ______ aa3 呀？

   A. gei2 • noi6 幾耐　　B. mei6 未　　C. jau5 mou5 有冇

3. *What is it?*

   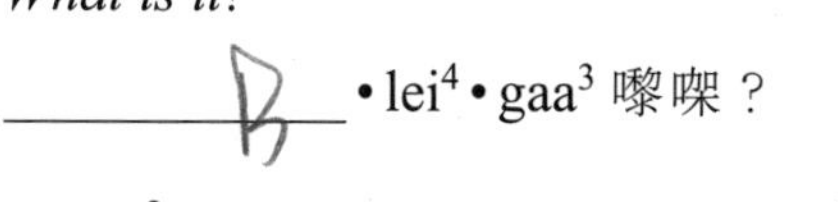
   ______ • lei4 • gaa3 嚟㗎？

   A. zo2 咗　　B. me1 咩　　C. mou5 冇

4. *I ate a sandwich.*

Ngo⁵ 我 sik⁶ 食 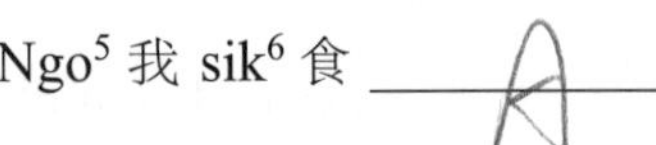 saam¹ • man⁴ • zi⁶ 三文治。

A. zo² 咗　　B. me¹ 咩　　C. mou⁵ 冇

5. *I have not eaten yet.*

Ngo⁵ 你 zung⁶ 仲 ________ sik⁶ • faan⁶ 食飯。

A. m⁴ 唔　　B. mou⁵ 冇　　C. mei⁶ 未

2.6.3 Fill in the number of the word given

A.	B.	C.	D.	E.
ge³ 嘅	zo² 咗	jan⁴ 人	hai² 喺	giu³ 叫
F.	**G.**	**H.**	**I.**	**J.**
siu² • siu² 少少	jyut⁶ 月	gong² 講	jau⁵ 有	hai⁶ 係

1. I am Japanese. My name is Haruko Katayama.
2. My Chinese name is 片山晴子 .
3. I have been in Hong Kong for 3 months.
4. I can speak Japanese, English and a little Cantonese.
5. I have two Hong Kong friends.

1. Ngo^5 ___J___ Jat^6 • bun^2 ___C___, ___E___ Haruko Katayama.
   我 ______ 日 本 ______，______ Haruko Katayama。

2. Ngo^5 ___A___ Zung^1 • man^4 meng^{2*} ___J___ Pin^3 • saan^1 Cing^4 • zi^2.
   我 ______ 中 文 名 ______ 片 山 晴 子。

3. Ngo^5 lei^4 ___B___ Hoeng^1 • gong^2 saam^1 go^3 ___G___.
   我 嚟 ______ 香 港 三 個 ______。

4. Ngo^5 sik^1 ___H___ Jat^6 • man^{2*}, Jing^1 • man^{2*} tung^4 (*and*) ___F___ Gwong^2 • dung^1 • waa^{2*}.
   我 識 ______ 日 文，英 文 同 ______ 廣 東 話。

5. Ngo^5 ___I___ loeng^5 go^3 Hoeng^1 • gong^2 pang^4 • jau^5.
   我 ______ 兩 個 香 港 朋 友。

3

Maai^5 • je^5

買 嘢 *Shopping*

Learning Tasks

- to ask about & indicate what to buy
- to talk about colors
- to ask about & indicate a price
- to bargain for a good price
- to ask for help

Grammar Notes

- classifiers (1)
- '*this, that, which*': ni^1 呢 , go^2 嗰 , bin^1 邊
- plural: di^1 啲
- '*how much*' questions: gei^2 • do^1 cin^{2*} 幾多錢
- '*how*' questions: dim^2 點
- adverb '*first*': sin^1 先
- giving someone something: bei^2 俾
- '*not only…but also…*': m^4• zi^2 唔止 …zung^6 仲 … tim^1 添

Sounds and Tones

- Cantonese long vowel "aa" & short vowel "a"

Supplementary Vocabulary

- numbers
- money
- colors
- clothing

Exercise

- matching
- multiple choice
- fill in the blanks

 3.1 Vocabulary *(Track 056)*

No.	Cantonese Romanization	Cantonese Characters	Putonghua & Chinese Characters	English
1.	Neoi5• jan2* Gaai1	女人街	Nǚrénjiē 女人街	Lady Market
2.	hou2 peng4	好平	hěn piányi 很便宜	very cheap
3.	a) di1	啲	xiē 些	plural marker, more
	b) (ni1) di1 je5	(呢)啲嘢	zhèxiē dōngxi 這些东西	(these) things, stuff
	c) peng4 di1	平啲	piányi diǎnr 便宜点儿	cheaper
4.	m4 • zi2…zung6…tim1	唔止…仲…添	búdàn 不但 … hái 还 … ne 呢	not only…but also …
5.	gam2	噉	nà 那	well, then
6.	gaau3	教	jiāo 教	teach
7.	dim2	點	zěnyàng 怎样	how
8.	gong2 • gaa3	講價	tǎo jià huán jià 讨价还价	bargain
9.	maai5	買	mǎi 买	buy
10.	a) ni1	呢	zhè 这	this
	b) ni1 gin6 Ti1 • seot1	呢件 T 恤	zhè jiàn Tī xù 这件 T 恤	this T-shirt
11.	haak1 • sik1	黑色	hēisè 黑色	black
12.	hou2 leng3	好靚	hěn piàoliang 很漂亮	very beautiful
13.	a) zi1	知	zhīdào 知道	know
	b) m4 zi1	唔知	bù zhīdào 不知道	don't know
	c) m4 zi1 gwai3 m4 gwai3	唔知貴唔貴	bù zhīdào guì bu guì 不知道贵不贵	don't know whether it's expensive or not
14.	a) bong1 nei5	幫你	bāng nǐ 帮你	help you / for you
	b) bong1 nei5 man6 • haa5	幫你問吓	tì nǐ wèn yíxià 替你问一下	ask on your behalf
	c) bong1 nei5 man6 • haa5 sin1	幫你問吓先	xiān tì nǐ wèn yíxià 先替你问一下	first ask on your behalf
15.	lou5 • baan2	老闆	lǎobǎn 老板	business owner, boss
16.	gei2 • do1 cin2*	幾多錢	duōshǎo qián 多少钱	how much (cost)
17.	a) man1	蚊	kuài 块	dollar(s)
	b) luk6 • sap6 man1	六十蚊	liù shí kuài 六十块	sixty dollars
18.	zau6	就	jiù 就	then / that

19.	gam^3 gwai^3	咁貴	zhème guì 这么贵	so expensive
20.	ji^5 • ging^1	已經	yǐjīng 已经	already
21.	a) go^2	嗰	nà 那	that
	b) go^2 gaan^1 pou^3 • tau^{2*}	嗰間舖頭	nà jiā diàn 那家店	that shop
22.	maai^6	賣	mài 卖	sell
23.	a) dak^1	得	xíng 行不行	okay
	b) m^4 dak^1	唔得	bùxíng 不行	not okay
	c) dak^1 m^4 dak^1	得唔得	xíng bùxíng 行不行	Is that okay?
24.	sit^6 • bun^2	蝕本	kuīběn 亏本	lose money
25.	syun^3 laa^1	算啦	suànle 算了	forget it
26.	zau^2 laa^3	走喇	zǒu ba 走吧	let's go
27.	faan^1 • lei^4	返嚟	huílái 回来	come back
28.	a) bei^2 … nei^5	俾…你	gěi nǐ 给你 …	give you ...
	b) bei^2 saam^1 gin^6 nei^5	俾三件你	gěi nǐ sān jiàn 给你三件	give you three (shirts)

3.2 Carmen takes Tai-Lung to Lady Market. *(Track 057)*

Neoi^5 • jan^{2*} Gaai^1 di^1 je^5 hai^6 m^4 hai^6 hou^2 peng^4 aa^3?
女 人 街 啲 嘢 係 唔 係 好 平 呀 ？
Are the things at Lady Market cheap or not?
女人街的东西是不是很便宜呢？

Neoi^5 • jan^{2*} Gaai^1 di^1 je^5 m^4 • zi^2 hou^2 peng^4, zung^6 ho^2 • ji^5 gong^2 • gaa^3 tim^1.
女 人 街 啲 嘢 唔 止 好 平 ，仲 可 以 講 價 添 。
Things at Lady Market are not only cheap, (but) you can also bargain down the prices.
女人街的东西不但便宜，还可以讨价还价呢！

Gam^2, nei^5 jiu^3 gaau^3 ngo^5 dim^2 gong^2 • gaa^3 laa^3.
噉 ，你 要 教 我 點 講 價 喇 。
Well, then you will have to teach me how to bargain prices.
那么，你要教我怎样讨价还价好了。

Nei^5 soeng^2 maai^5 di^1 me^1 aa^3?
你 想 買 啲 咩 呀 ？
What do you want to buy?
你想买些什么呢？

Ngo^{5} soeng^{2} maai^{5} di^{1} Ti^{1} • seot^{1}.
我 想 買 啲 T 恤 。
I want to buy some shirts.
我想买些T恤。

Tai-Lung looks through the rack of T shirts.

Ni^{1} gin^{6} haak^{1} • sik^{1} ge^{3} Ti^{1} • seot^{1} hou^{2} leng^{3}, m^{4} zi^{1} gwai^{3} m^{4} gwai^{3} ne^{1}?
呢 件 黑 色 嘅 T 恤 好 靚 ， 唔 知 貴 唔 貴 呢 ？
This black shirt is very nice. I don't know whether it is expensive or not?
这件黑色的T恤很漂亮，不知道贵不贵？

Ngo^{5} bong^{1} nei^{5} man^{6} • haa^{5} sin^{1}.
我 幫 你 問 吓 先 。
Let me ask for you.
我先替你问一下。

M^{4} • goi^{1}!
唔 該 ！
Thank you!
谢谢！

Lou^{5} • baan^{2}, ni^{1} gin^{6} Ti^{1} • seot^{1} gei^{2} • do^{1} cin^{2*} aa^{3}?
老 闆 ， 呢 件 T 恤 幾 多 錢 呀 ？
How much is this shirt?
老板，这件T恤多少钱？

Luk^{6} • sap^{6} man^{1}.
六 十 蚊 。
60 dollars.
六十块。

Waa^{4}! Gam^{3} gwai^{3}! Peng^{4} di^{1} laa^{1}.
嘩 ！ 咁 貴 ！ 平 啲 啦 。
Wow! That's so expensive! Can't you make it a little cheaper?
哇！这么贵！便宜点吧。

M^{4} gwai^{3} laa^{3}, ji^{5} • ging^{1} hou^{2} peng^{4} laa^{3}.
唔 貴 喇 ， 已 經 好 平 喇 。
This is'nt expensive. It's already quite cheap.
不贵，已经很便宜了。

Go2 gaan1 maai6 sei3 • sap6 man1, nei5 maai6 luk6 • sap6 man1?
嗰 間 舖 頭 賣 四 十 蚊 ， 你 賣 六 十 蚊 ？
They sell it for $40 over there at that store. Are you telling me your're selling it for $60?
那家店卖四十块，你卖六十块？

Hou2 laa1, sei3 sap6 zau6 sei3 • sap6 laa1.
好 啦 ， 四 十 就 四 十 啦 。
Okay, let's make it $40.
好的，四十就四十吧。

Ngo5 soeng2 maai5 saam1 gin6.
我 想 買 三 件 。
I want to buy three (of them).
我想买三件。

Lou5 • baan2, jat1 • baak3 man1 saam1 gin6, dak1 m4 dak1 aa3?
老 闆 ， 一 百 蚊 三 件 ， 得 唔 得 呀 ？
Hey mister, $100 for three, (how's that)is that okay?
老板，一百块三件，好吗？

M4 dak1, ngo5 jiu3 sit6 • bun2 laa3.
唔 得 ， 我 要 蝕 本 喇 。
No, I would lost money.
不成，我要亏本了。

Gam2, syun3 laa1, zau2 laa3.
噉 ， 算 啦 ， 走 喇 。
Then forget it, let's go.
那么算了，走吧。

Faan1 • lei4, faan1 • lei4, jat1 • baak3 man1 bei2 saam1 gin6 nei5 laa1.
返 嚟 、 返 嚟 ， 一 百 蚊 俾 三 件 你 啦 。
Come back, come back. I'll give you three for $100.
回来，回来，一百块给你们三件吧。

3.3 Grammar Notes

3.3.1 Classifiers (1) *(Track 058)*

When indicating the number of a person, or thing etc., a classifier has to be placed between the number (see 3.5.1) and the noun. Note that Cantonese classifiers are often different from those of Putonghua.

go3	個	a general classifier for people, places, families, round objects, etc.
gin6	件	for upper clothing, pieces of cake, matters, etc.
tiu4	條	for long & thin objects, such as streets, pants, ties, fish, etc.
zi1	枝	for long & thin objects that are relatively small, such as pens, bottles, cigarettes, etc.
bun2	本	for books, notebooks, magazines, etc.
zek3	隻	for animals, body parts, CD's, windows, songs, etc.
deoi3	對	for paired objects, paired body parts, couples, etc.
zoeng1	張	for flat objects, such as paper, beds, tables, chairs, cards, etc.
gaan1	間	for rooms, buildings, shops, etc.
ceot1	齣	for movies, plays, etc.

Examples:

C	P	E
jat1 go3 jan4 一個人	yí ge rén 一个人	a person
jat1 gin6 saam1 一件衫	yí jiàn yīfu 一件衣服	a shirt
jat1 tiu4 fu3 一條褲	yì tiáo kùzi 一条裤子	a pair of pants
jat1 zi1 bat1 一枝筆	yì zhī bǐ 一枝笔	a pen
jat1 bun2 syu1 一本書	yì běn shū 一本书	a book
jat1 zek3 CD 一隻 CD	yì zhāng guāngdié 一张光盘	a CD
jat1 deoi3 haai4 一對鞋	yì shuāng xié 一双鞋	a pair of shoes
jat1 zoeng1 zi2 一張紙	yì zhāng zhǐ 一张纸	a piece of paper
jat1 gaan1 daai6 • hok6 一間大學	yì suǒ dàxué 一所大学	a university
jat1 ceot1 hei3 一齣戲	yí bù xì 一部电影	a movie

3.3.2 This, that and which : ni¹ 呢，go² 嗰，bin¹ 邊 (Track 059)

'*This*' and '*that*' are expressed with "ni¹ 呢" and "go² 嗰" respectively. When asking '*which*', "bin¹ 邊" is used. Unlike Putonghua, "ni¹ 呢", "go² 嗰" and "bin¹ 邊" must be followed by a classifier (see 3.3.1).

P zhè 這、nà 那、nǎ 哪

Examples:

1. Bin¹ bun² syu¹ hou² aa³?
   邊 本 書 好 呀 ？
   Which book is good?
   哪本书好？

2. Ni¹ bun² hou².
   呢 本 好 。
   This one is good.
   这本好。

3.3.3 Plural : di¹ 啲 (Track 060)

"Di¹ 啲" is a plural classifier similar to xiē 些 in Putonghua. To express '*these*' and '*those*', "ni¹ di¹ 呢啲" and "go² di¹ 嗰啲" are used respectively.

P xiē 些

Examples:

1. Ni¹ di¹ je⁵ hou² gwai³.
   呢 啲 嘢 好 貴 。
   These things are so expensive.
   这些东西很贵。

2. Go² di¹ neoi⁵ • zai² hou² leng³.
   嗰 啲 女 仔 好 靚 。
   Those girls are very pretty.
   那些女孩子很漂亮。

3.3.4 '*How much*' guestions: gei² • do¹ cin²* 幾多錢 (Track 061)

'*How many / much*' is expressed with "gei² • do¹ 幾多", equivalent to duōshǎo 多少 in Putonghua. When asking the amount of money, "gei² • do¹ cin²* 幾多錢" is used.

P duōshǎo qián 多少钱

Examples:

1. *A:* Ni1 • go3 gei2 • do1 cin2* aa3?
呢 個 幾 多 錢 呀 ？
How much is this one?
这个 多少钱？

B: Ji6 • sap6 man1.
二 十 蚊 。
Twenty dollars.
二十块钱。

2. *A:* Nei5 jau5 gei2 • do1 cin2* aa3?
你 有 幾 多 錢 呀 ？
How much money do you have?
你有多少钱？

B: Jat1 • baak3 man1.
一 百 蚊 。
One hundred dollars.
一百块钱。

3.3.5 '*How*' guestions: dim2 點 *(Track 062)*

"Dim2 點" is used before a verb phrase to ask the way something is done. Unlike English, there is no need for "dim2" to be placed in the sentence initial position.

P zěnyàng 怎样 / zěnme 怎么

Examples:

1. *A:* 'Good morning' Gwong2 • dung1 • waa2* dim2 gong2 aa3?
'Good morning' 廣 東 話 點 講 呀 ？
How do you say 'good morning' in Cantonese?
'早上好' 广东话怎么说？

B: Jou2 • san4.
早 晨 。
Good morning.
早上好。

2. *A:* Dim2 heoi3 Laan4 • gwai3 • fong1 aa3?
點 去 蘭 桂 坊 呀 ？
How can I get to Lan Kwai Fong?
兰桂坊怎么走？

B: Daap3 dei6 • tit3
搭 地 鐵 。
Take the MTR.
坐地铁。

3.3.6 Adverb '*first*' : sin1 先 *(Track 063)*

"Sin1 先" is placed after a verb phrase, meaning '*first*'.

Examples:

1. Nei5 haang4 sin1 laa1.
你 行 先 啦 。
You go first.
你先走吧。

2. Ngo5 zau2 sin1 laa3.
我 走 先 喇 。
I'll leave first (before you).
我先走了。

3.3.7 Give someone something : bei² 俾 (Track 064)

The '*give*'' expression takes the order of "bei² 俾 *(give)* + something 嘢 *(thing)* + jan⁴ 人 *(person)*". Note that something and someone are placed in the reverse order from those in Putonghua.

P gěi 给

Examples:

1. Nei⁵ bei² cin²* ngo⁵.
   你 俾 錢 我 。
   You give me money.
   你给我钱。

2. Ngo⁵ bei² • zo² jat¹ bun² syu¹ keoi⁵.
   我 俾 咗 一 本 書 佢 。
   I gave a book to him.
   我给了他一本书。

3.3.8 To express '*not only...but also*' : m⁴ • zi² 唔止 ... zung⁶ 仲 ... tim¹ 添 (Track 065)

To express '*not only* A, *but also* B', "m⁴ • zi² 唔止 + A + zung⁶ 仲 + B + tim¹ 添" is used, where A & B are verb or adjective phrases.

P búdàn...hái / yě...
不但…还 / 也…

Examples:

1. Keoi⁵ m⁴ • zi² sik¹ gong² Jing¹ • man²*, zung⁶ sik¹ gong² Gwong² • dung¹ • waa²* tim¹.
   佢 唔 止 識 講 英 文 ， 仲 識 講 廣 東 話 添 。
   She can not only speak English, but also Cantonese.
   她不但会说英文，还会说广东话。

2. Nei⁵ m⁴ • zi² hou² leng³, zung⁶ hou² hou² • jan⁴ tim¹.
   你 唔 止 好 靚 ， 仲 好 好 人 添 。
   You are not only very beautiful, but also kind-hearted.
   你不但很漂亮，心眼也很好。

3.4 Cantonese long "aa" and short "a"

Cantonese differentiates long "aa" and short "a". To grasp the difference effectively, you can compare "aa" and "a" together with the following vowels and consonants.

Listen carefully and mimic the following minimal pairs.

(a) aai - ai *(Track 066)*

1.	gaai^1	街	street	gai^1	雞	chicken
2.	saai^3	晒	very much	sai^3	細	small

(b) aau - au *(Track 067)*

1.	caau^2	炒	fry	cau^2	醜	ugly
2.	haau^2	考	exam	hau^2	口	mouth

(c) aam - am *(Track 068)*

1.	gaam^2	減	subtract	gam^2	敢	dare
2.	caam^1	參	join	cam^1	侵	invade

(d) aan - an *(Track 069)*

1.	maan^6	慢	slow	man^6	問	ask
2.	waan^2	玩	play	wan^2	搵	look for

(e) aang - ang *(Track 070)*

1.	saang^1	生	lively	sang^1	生	life
2.	haang^4	行	walk	hang^4	恆	forever

(f) aap - ap *(Track 071)*

1.	zaap^6	習	study	zap^1	汁	juice
2.	haap^6	狹	narrow	hap^6	合	close

(g) aat - at *(Track 072)*

1.	baat^3	八	eight	bat^1	筆	pen
2.	caat^3	擦	erase	cat^1	七	seven

(h) aak - ak *(Track 073)*

1.	baak^3	百	hundred	bak^1	北	north
2.	caak^6	賊	thief	cak^1	測	survey

3.5 Supplementary Vocabulary

3.5.1 Numbers

(a) 0 – 10 *(Track 074)*

0	ling^4	3	saam^1	6	luk^6	9	gau^2
1	jat^1	4	sei^3	7	cat^1	10	sap^6
2	ji^6	5	ng^5	8	baat^3		

(b) 11 – 19 *(Track 075)* Formula: "sap^6" + n_{1-9}, e.g. to say 13, simply say 10 + 3.

11	sap^6 • jat^1	14	sap^6• sei^4	17	sap^6• cat^1	
12	sap^6 • ji^6	15	sap^6• ng^5	18	sap^6• baat^3	
13	sap^6 • saam^1	16	sap^6• luk^6	19	sap^6• gau^2	

(c) 20 – 100 *(Track 076)* N.B. Formula: "n_{1-9} × sap^6" (+ n_{1-9}), e.g. to say 36, simply say 3+10+ 6. When sap^6 is followed by n_{1-9}, it is simplified to aa^6. Also "ji^6 • sap^6 *(20)*" and "saam^1 • sap^6 *(30)*" often becomes jaa^6 and saa^1 • aa^6 when followed by n_{1-9}.

20	ji^6 • sap^6	43	sei^3 • aa^6 • saam^1	76	cat^1 • aa^6 • luk^6	99	gau^2 • aa^6 • gau^2
21	jaa^6 • jat^1	54	ng^5 • aa^6 • sei^3	87	baat^3 • aa^6 • cat^1	100	jat^1 • baak^3
32	saa^1 • aa^6 • ji^6	65	luk^6 • aa^6 • ng^5	98	gau^2 • aa^6 • baat^3		

(d) Lucky and unlucky numbers in Cantonese *(Track 077)*

Lucky:

"ji^6 二 *(two)* " :	same as	"ji^6 易 *(easily)*".
"saam^1 三 *(three)*" :	similar to	"saang^1 生 *(lively)*".
"baat^3 八 *(eight)*" :	similar to	"faat^3 發 *(prosperous)*".
"gau^2 九 *(nine)*" :	same as	"gau^2 久 *(long lasting)*".

Unlucky:

"sei^3 四 *(four)*" :	similar to	"sei^2 死 *(death)*".
"sap^6 • sei^3 十四 *(fourteen)*" :	similar to	"sat^6 • sei^2 實死 *(die for sure)*".

 3.5.2 Money

(a) Cents and dollars *(Track 078)*

10¢	jat^{1} hou^{4} 一毫	$10	sap^{6} man^{1} 十蚊
20¢	loeng^{5} hou^{4} 兩毫	$20	ji^{6} • sap^{6} man^{1} 二十蚊
50¢	ng^{5} hou^{4} 五毫	$30	ng^{5} • sap^{6} man^{1} 五十蚊
$1	jat^{1} man^{1} 一蚊	$100	jat^{1} • baak^{3} man^{1} 一百蚊
$2	loeng^{5} man^{1} 兩蚊	$500	ng^{5} • baak^{3} man^{1} 五百蚊
$5	ng^{5} man^{1} 五蚊	$1000	jat^{1} • cin^{1} man^{1} 一千蚊

†† "Loeng^{5}" is used before "man^{1} *(dollar)*" and "hou^{4} *(cents)*" instead of "ji^{6}".

(b) Cents and dollars in short form *(Track 079)*

In colloquial speech, "go^{3} 個" is used to refer to the decimal point without expressing "man^{1} 蚊 *(dollar)*" and "hou^{4} 毫 *(cents)*" (see below). 50 cents is often referred to as "bun^{3} 半 *(half)*" when used after "go^{3} 個 *(short form for dollar)*". The number "jat^{1} 一 *(one)*" is dropped when used before "go^{3} 個" as in "go^{3} • saam^{1} 個三 *($1.3)*".

$1.2	go^{3} • ji^{6}	$11.8	sap^{6} • jat^{1} • go^{3} • baat^{3}
$2.5	loeng^{5} • go^{3} • bun^{3}	$68.7	luk^{6} • aa^{6} • baat^{3} • go^{3} • cat^{1}
$9.9	gau^{2} • go^{3} • gau^{2}	$93.1	gau^{2} • aa^{6} • saam^{1} • go^{3} • jat^{1}

(c) 101 – 10,000 dollars *(Track 080)*

$101	jat^{1} • baak^{3} ling^{4} jat^{1} man^{1}	$1,000	jat^{1} • cin^{1} man^{1}
$234	ji^{6} • baak^{3} saa^{1} • aa^{6} • sei^{3} man^{1}	$2,985	ji^{6} • cin^{1} gau^{2} • baak^{3} baat^{3} • aa^{6} • ng^{5} man^{1}
$567	ng^{5} • baak^{3} luk^{6} • aa^{6} • cat^{1} man^{1}	$10,000	jat^{1} • maan^{6} man^{1}

3.5.3 Color *(Track 081)*

No.	Cantonese Romanization	Chinese	Putonghua Romanization	Common spellings used in Hong Kong
1.	laam^{4} • sik^{1}	藍色	lánsè 蓝色	blue
2.	fe^{1} • sik^{1}	啡色	kāfēi sè 咖啡色 / zōngsè 棕色	brown
3.	fui^{1} • sik^{1}	灰色	huīsè 灰色	gray
4.	luk^{6} • sik^{1}	綠色	lǜsè 绿色	green
5.	caang^{2} • sik^{1}	橙色	chéngsè 橙色	orange
6.	fan^{2} • hung^{4} • sik^{1}	粉紅色	fěnhóngsè 粉红色	pink
7.	zi^{2} • sik^{1}	紫色	zǐsè 紫色	purple
8.	hung^{4} • sik^{1}	紅色	hóngsè 红色	red
9.	baak^{6} • sik^{1}	白色	báisè 白色	white
10.	wong^{4} • sik^{1}	黃色	huángsè 黄色	yellow

3.5.4 Clothing *(Track 082)*

No.	Cantonese Romanization	Chinese	Putonghua Romanization	Common spellings used in Hong Kong
1.	ngau^{4} • zai^{2} • fu^{3}	牛仔褲	niúzǎikù 牛仔裤	jeans
2.	tou^{3} • zong^{1}	套裝	tàozhuāng 套装	ladies' suits
3.	pei^{4} • haai^{4}	皮鞋	pixie 皮鞋	leather shoes
4.	sai^{1} • zong^{1}	西裝	xīzhuāng 西装	men's suits
5.	fu^{3}	褲	kùzi 裤子	pants
6.	seot^{1} • saam^{1}	恤衫	chènshān 衬衫	shirt
7.	kwan^{4}	裙	qúnzi 裙子	skirt
8.	mat^{6}	襪	wàzi 袜子	socks
9.	wan^{6} • dung^{6} saam^{1}	運動衫	yùndòngfú 运动服	sports shirt
10.	wan^{6} • dung^{6} haai^{4}	運動鞋	yùndòngxié 运动鞋	sports shoes

3.6 Exercise

3.6.1 Matching

1. jat^1 一 ( ) syu^1 書 *book*
2. jat^1 一 ( ) fong^{2*} 房 *room*
3. jat^1 一 ( ) caang^2 橙 *orange*
4. jat^1 一 ( ) seot^1 • saam^1 恤衫 *shirt*
5. jat^1 一 ( ) ngau^4 • zai^2 • fu^3 牛仔褲 *jeans*

A. go^3 個
B. tiu^4 條
C. gin^6 件
D. gaan^1 間
E. bun^2 本

3.6.2 Multiple choice

1. *He gave me a bottle of Coke.*
   Keoi^5 佢 __________ zo^2 咗 jat^1 一 zi^1 枝 ho^2 • lok^6 可樂 ngo^5 我。

   A. bin^1 邊　　B. di^1 啲　　C. bei^2 俾

2. *How much do you have?*
   Nei^5 你 jau^5 有 __________ cin^{2*} 錢 aa^3 呀？

   A. m^4 • zi^2 唔止　　B. gei^2 • do^1 幾多　　C. dim^2 點

3. *How do you say "apple" in Cantonese?*
   'Apple' Gwong^2 • dung^1 • waa^{2*} 廣東話 __________ gong^2 講 aa^3 呀？

   A. sin^1 先　　B. dim^2 點　　C. me^1 咩

4. *These computers are so expensive.*
   Ni^1 呢 __________ din^6 • nou^5 電腦 hou^2 好 gwai^3 貴。

   A. di^1 啲　　B. go^2 嗰　　C. mou^5 冇

5. *Goods in Hong Kong are not only cheap, but also nice-looking.*
   Hoeng^1 • gong^2 香港 ge^3 嘅 je^5 嘢 __________ hou^2 好 peng^4 平 zung^6 仲 hou^2 好 leng^3 靚 tim^1 添。

   A. m^4 hou^2 唔好　　B. gei^2 • do^1 幾多　　C. m^4 • zi^2 唔止

3.6.3 Fill in the number for the phrase given

A.	jaa6 • sei3 man1	B.	jat1 • maan6 cat1 • cin1 man1
C.	sap6 • cat1 • go3 • bun3	D.	saam1 • cin1 man1
E.	ng5 • baak3 gau2 • sap6 man1	F.	jat1 • baak3 luk6 • sap6 • baat3 man1
G.	jat1 • cin1 luk6 • baak3 man1	H.	ji6 • baak3 saam1 • sap6 man1
I.	go3 • saam1	J.	gau2 • aa3 • gau2 man1

1.

bat1
筆
$ 1.3
(I)

2.

saam1 • man4 • zi6
三文治
$ 17.5
(C)

3.

bou2
簿
$ 24
(A)

4.

syu1
書
$ 1,600
(G)

5.

toi2
枱
$ 590
(E)

6.

haai4
鞋
$ 230
(H)

7.

saam1
衫
$ 168
(F)

8.

fu3
褲
$ 99
(J)

9.

gaai3 • zi2
戒指
$ 17,000
(B)

10.

din6 • nou5
電腦
$ 3,000
(D)

4 Haau^{6} • jyun^{4} sang^{1} • wut^{6}

校園生活 *Campus life*

Learning Tasks

- to ask for directions (2)
- to recognize the location of school facilities
- to ask about & indicate a reason
- to recognize clock hour
- to describe daily routine
- to ask about & indicate a weekly schedule
- to talk about a sequence of actions

Grammar Notes

- conjunction '*and*': tung^{4} 同
- direction-giving
- time segment expressions
- clock time: dim^{2} 點
- '*why*' questions: dim^{2} • gaai^{2} 點解
- a series of events: … sin^{1} 先 , gan^{1} • zyu^{6} 跟住 …
- word order (1)

Sounds and Tones

- Similar-sounding finals

Supplementary Vocabulary

- days of the week
- school facilities
- meals
- daily activities

Exercise

- matching
- multiple choice
- fill in the blanks

4.1 Vocabulary *(Track 083)*

No.	Cantonese Romanization	Cantonese Characters	Putonghua & Chinese Characters	English
1.	tai^2 • juk^6 • gun^2	體育館	tǐyùguǎn 体育馆	gymnasium
2.	tung^4	同	hé 和 / gēn 跟	and
3.	wan^6 • dung^6 • coeng^4	運動場	yùndòngchǎng 运动场	sports ground
4.	ngan^4 • hong^4	銀行	yínháng 银行	bank
5.	jat^1 • zik^6 haang^4	一直行	yìzhí zǒu 一直走	go straight ahead
6.	cin^4 • min^6 / cin^4 • bin^6	前面 / 前便	qiánmiàn 前面	in front
7.	zyun^3 zo^2	轉左	zuǒ guǎi 左拐	turn left
8.	gaak^3 • lei^4	隔籬	gébì 隔壁	next to
9.	deoi^3 • min^6	對面	duìmiàn 对面	opposite of
10.	gei^2 daai^6	幾大	tǐng dà 挺大	quite big
11.	zi^1 laa^3	知喇	zhīdàole 知道了	got it (I now know)
12.	tou^4 • syu^1 • gun^2	圖書館	túshūguǎn 图书馆	library
13.	a) … me^1?	…咩？	…ma 吗？	…isn't it?
	b) m^4 hai^6 jiu^3 soeng^5 • tong^4 me^1?	唔係要上堂咩？	búshì yào shàngkè ma? 不是要上课吗？	don't you have class?
	c) hou^2 je^6 fan^3 me^1?	好夜瞓咩？	hěn wǎn shuì ma? 很晚睡吗？	did you stay up very late?
14.	a) lai^5 • baai^3 • jat^1	禮拜一	lǐbài yī 礼拜一	Monday
	b) lai^5 • baai^3 • sei^3	禮拜四	lǐbài sì 礼拜四	Thursday
	c) lai^5 • baai^3 • jat^1 dou^3 lai^5 • baai^3 • sei^3	禮拜一到禮拜四	lǐbài yī dào lǐbài sì 礼拜一到礼拜四	from Monday to Thursday
15.	a) jat^6	日	tiān 天	day
	b) mui^5 jat^6	每日	měi tiān 每天	every day
	c) gam^1 • jat^6	今日	jīntiān 今天	today
	d) kam^4 • jat^6	琴日	zuótiān 昨天	yesterday
16.	a) ziu^1 • zou^2	朝早	zǎoshang 早上	morning
	b) aan^3 • zau^3	晏晝	zhōngwǔ / xiàwǔ 中午 / 下午	noon / afternoon

	c) je6 • maan5	夜晚	wǎnshang 晚上	night
	d) bun3 • je2*	半夜	bànyè 半夜	middle of the night
17.	a) gam1 • maan5 / gam1 • maan1*	今晚	jīntiān wǎnshang 今天晚上	tonight
	b) kam4 • maan5	琴晚	zuótiān wǎnshang 昨天晚上	last night
18.	a) gei2 dim2	幾點？	jǐ diǎn 几点	what's the time?
	b) sap6 • ji6 dim2	十二點	shí èr diǎn 十二点	twelve o'clock
19.	a) hei2 • san1	起身	qǐchuáng 起床	get up
	b) hou2 aan3 hei2 • san1	好晏起身	hěn wǎn qǐchuáng 很晚起床	get up very late
20.	a) fan3 • gaau3	瞓覺	shuìjiào 睡觉	sleep
	b) hou2 je6 fan3	好夜瞓	hěn wǎn shuìjiào 很晚睡觉	stay up late
21.	zou2-seoi6-zou2-hei2	早睡早起	zǎoshuìzǎoqǐ 早睡早起	early keep early hours
22.	lin6 gung1 • fu1	練功夫	liàn gōngfu 练功夫	practice martial art
23.	…sin1, gan1 • zyu6	…先，跟住	xiān 先 … jiēzhe 接着	first…and then
24.	cung1 • loeng4	沖涼	xǐzǎo 洗澡	take a bath
25.	sik6 zou2 • caan1	食早餐	chī zǎofàn 吃早饭	eat breakfast
26.	dim2• gaai2	點解	wèi shénme 为什么	why
27.	heoi3 Laan4 • gwai3 • fong1 jam2 • zau2	去蘭桂坊飲酒	qù Lánguìfāng hē jiǔ 去兰桂坊喝酒	go and drink in Lan Kwai Fong
28.	a) tong4	堂	kè 课	class
	b) soeng5 • tong4	上堂	shàng kè 上课	go to class
	c) lok6 • tong4	落堂	xià kè 下课	get off from class
	d) jau5 tong4	有堂	yǒu kè 有课	have classes
	e) mou5 tong4	冇堂	méiyǒu kè 没有课	have no classes

4.2 Ka-Man brings Tai-Lung to walk around the campus. *(Track 084)*

Tai2 • juk6 • gun2 tung4 wan6 • dung6 • coeng4 hai2 bin1 • dou6 aa3?
體育館同運動場喺邊度呀 ?
Where are the gymnasium and the sports ground?
体育馆和运动场在哪儿？

Cin4 • min6 zau6 • hai6 laa3.
前面就係喇 。
They are just in front of us (They are just down the road).
前面就是了。

Ni1 go6 wan6 • dung6 • coeng4 gei2 daai6 wo3.
呢個運動場幾大喎 。
The sports ground is quite big.
这个运动场挺大的啊。

Jat1 • zik6 haang4, haang4 dou3 dai6-jat1 go3 lou6 • hau2 zyun3 zo2 zau6 • hai6 tai2 • juk6 • gun2 laa3.
一直行，行到第一個路口轉左就係體育館喇 。
Go straight until the first corner, and turn left, then you'll see a gymnasium.
一直走，走到第一个路口左拐就是体育馆了。

Zi1 laa3, m4 • goi1. Tou4 • syu1 • gun2 tung4 ngan4 • hong4 hai2 bin1 • dou6 aa3?
知喇，唔該 。圖書館同銀行喺邊度呀 ?
Got it, thanks. Where are the library and the computer center located?
知道了，谢谢。图书馆和银行呢？

Tou4 • syu1 • gun2 hai2 tai2 • juk6 • gun2 gaak3 • lei4, ngan4 • hong4 hai2 tai2 • juk6 • gun2 deoi3• min6.
圖書館喺體育館隔籬，銀行喺體育館對面 。
The library is next to the gymnasium and the bank is opposite of the gymnasium.
图书馆在体育馆的旁边，银行在体育馆的对面。

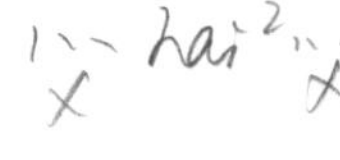

Ka-Man and Tai-Lung bumped into Ka-Nam in the computer center.

Nei5 m4 hai6 jiu3 soeng5 • tong4 me1? Dim2 • gaai2 nei5 hai2 ni1 • dou6 aa3?
你唔係要上堂咩 ？點解你喺呢度呀 ？
Don't you have class? How come you are here?
你不是要上课吗？为什么你在这里？

Kam4 • maan5 ngo5 tung4 pang4 • jau5 heoi3 Laan4 • gwai3 • fong1 jam2 • zau2.
琴 晚 我 同 朋 友 去 蘭 桂 坊 飲 酒 。
I had some drinks at Lan Kwai Fong last night with my friends.
昨天晚上我跟朋友去兰桂坊喝酒，所以很晚起床。

Nei5 hou2 je6 fan3 me1?
你 好 夜 瞓 咩 ？
Did you stay up very late?
你睡得很晚吗？

Ngo5 bun3 • je2* sei3 dim2 fan3. Nei5 • dei6 ping4 • si4 gei2 dim2 fan3 • gaau3 aa3?
我 半 夜 四 點 瞓 。 你 哋 平 時 幾 點 瞓 覺 呀 ？
I went to bed at four past mid-night. What time do you guys usually go to bed?
我半夜四点睡觉。你们平时几点睡觉啊？

Ngo5 ping4 • si4 je6 • maan5 sap6 • ji6 dim2 fan3, ziu1 • zou2 baat3 dim2 hei2 • san1.
我 平 時 夜 晚 十 二 點 瞓 ， 朝 早 八 點 起 身 。
Usually I go to bed at twelve at night and get up at eight in the morning.
我平时晚上十二点睡觉，早上八点起来。

Ngo5 zaap6 • gwaan3 zou2 - seoi6 - zou2 - hei2, sap6 • dim2 fan3 • gaau3, luk6 dim2 hei2 • san1.
我 習 慣 早 睡 早 起 ， 十 點 瞓 覺 ， 六 點 起 身 。
I am used to keeping early hours. I go to bed at ten and get up at six.
我习惯早睡觉早起床，十点睡觉，六点起床。

Nei5 luk6 dim2 hei2 • san1?
你 六 點 起 身 ？
Are you saying that you get up at six?
你六点起床嘛？

Lin6 gung1 • fu1 sin1, gan1 • zyu6 cung1 • loeng4, sik6 zou2 • caan1, soeng5 • tong4.
練 功 夫 先 ， 跟 住 沖 涼 、 食 早 餐 、 上 堂 。
I'll practice martial arts first, then I'll take a bath, eat breakfast and go to class.
先练功夫，接着洗澡、吃早饭、上课。

Nei5 • dei6 mui5 • jat6 dou1 jau5 tong4 me1?
你 哋 每 日 都 有 堂 咩 ？
Do you have classes every day?
你们每天都有课吗？

Ngo^5 lai^5 • baai^3 • jat^1 dou^3 lai^5• baai^3 • sei^3 dou^1 jau^5 tong^4.
我 禮 拜 一 到 禮 拜 四 都 有 堂 。
I have classes from Monday to Thursday.
我礼拜一到礼拜四都有课。

Ngo^5 dou^1 hai^6.
我 都 係 。
Me, too.
我也是。

Gaa^1 • naam^4, nei^5 ne^1?
家男 ， 你 呢 ？
Ka-Nam, how about you?
家男，你呢？

Ngo^5 mui^5 jat^6 dou^1 jau^5 tong^4.
我 每 日 都 有 堂 。
I have classes every day.
我每天都有课。

4.3 Grammar Notes

4.3.1 Conjunction 'and' : tung^4 同 *(Track 085)*

"Tung^4 同" means '*and*' or '*with*'.

P hé 和

Examples:

1. Ngo^5 tung^4 keoi^5 dou^1 zyu^6 hai^2 suk^1 • se^3.
   我 同 佢 都 住 喺 宿 舍 。
   She and I both live in the hostel.
   我和她都住在宿舍。

2. Ngo^5 soeng^2 sik^6 haa^1 • gaau^2 tung^4 siu^1 • maai^2*.
   我 想 食 蝦 餃 同 燒 賣 。
   I would like to have shrimp dumpling and pork dumpling.
   我想吃虾饺和烧卖。

4.3.2 Direction-giving : *(Track 086)*

The following phrases are often used when you ask for directions.

C	P	E
jat^{1} • zik^{6} haang^{4} 一直行	yīzhí zǒu 一直走	go straight ahead
zyun^{3} • waan^{1} 轉彎	zhuǎnwān 转弯	turn
zyun^{3} zo^{2} 轉左	zuǒ guǎi 左拐	turn left
zyun^{3} jau^{6} 轉右	yòu guǎi 右拐	turn right
hai^{2} cin^{4} • min^{6} 喺前面	zài qiánmiàn 在前面	in front (down the road)
hai^{2} gaak^{3} • lei^{4} 喺隔籬	zài gébì 在隔壁	next-door
hai^{2} deoi^{3} • min^{6} 喺對面	zài duìmiàn 在对面	opposite of
m^{4} zi^{1} • dou^{3} 唔知道	bù zhīdào 不知道	don't know

Examples:

1. Ceng^{2} • man^{6} syu^{1} • guk^{2*} hai^{2} bin^{1} • dou^{6} aa^{3}?
   請 問 書 局 喺 邊 度 呀 ？
   May I ask where the book store is?
   请问书店在哪儿？

2. Jat^{1} • zik^{6} haang^{4}, haang^{4} dou^{3} Mak^{6} • dong^{1} • lou^{4} zyun^{3} jau^{6}.
   一 直 行 ， 行 到 麥 當 勞 轉 右 。
   Go straight. Turn right when you McDonald's.
   一直走，走到麦当劳右拐。

4.3.3 Time segment expressions : *(Track 087)*

Cantonese divides a day into five time segments.

C	P	E
ziu^{1} • zou^{2} 朝早	zǎoshang 早上	morning
zung^{1} • ng^{5} 中午	zhōngwǔ 中午	noon
aan^{3} • zau^{3} 晏晝	xiàwǔ 下午	afternoon
je^{6} • maan^{5} 夜晚	wǎnshàng 晚上	night
bun^{3} • je^{2*} 半夜	bànyè 半夜	midnight

Examples:

1. *A:* Nei^5 ziu^1 • zou^2 mou^5 sik^6 zou^2 • caan^1, ngo^6 m^4 ngo^6 aa^3?
你 朝 早 有 食 早 餐 ， 餓 唔 餓 呀 ？
You didn't have breakfast this morning. Aren't you hungry?
你早上没有吃早饭，肚子餓嗎？

B: M^4 ngo^6.
唔 餓 。
Not hungry.
不餓。

2. Ngo^5 aan^3 • zau^3 mou^5 tong^4, je^6 • maan^5 jau^5 tong^4.
我 晏 晝 冇 堂 ， 夜 晚 有 堂 。
I have no afternoon classes, but I have evening classes.
我下午没课，晚上有课。

4.3.4 Clock hour : dim^2 點 (Track 088)

A number plus "dim^2 點 *(o'clock)*" is used to form a clock hour expression, e.g. "loeng^5 dim^2 兩點 *(2 o'clock)*". When asking the time, "gei^2 dim^2 幾點" is used. Unlike English, the time expression is placed before a verb phrase to indicate the time you do something.

Examples:

1. *A:* Ji^4 • gaa^1 gei^2 dim^2 aa^3?
而 家 幾 點 呀 ？
What time is it now?
现在几点？

B: Saam^1 dim^2.
三 點 。
Three o'clock.
三点钟。

2. Ngo^5 saam^1 dim^2 soeng^5 • tong^4.
我 三 點 上 堂 。
I have class at three o'clock.
我三点钟上课。

†† 2 o'clock is "*loeng^5 dim^2*". 12 o'clock is "*sap^6 • yi^6 dim^2*".

4.3.5 '*Why*' questions : dim^2 • gaai^2 點解 (Track 089)

To ask the reason for something, "dim^2 • gaai^2 點解" is used right before a verb / adjective phrase or before a subject. To explain the reason, use "jan^1 • wai^6 因為 *(because)*" (see 9.3.5).

P wèishénme 为什么

Examples:

1. Keoi^5 dim^2 • gaai^2 ci^4 • dou^3 aa^3?
佢 點 解 遲 到 呀 ？
Why was he late?
他为什么迟到？

2. Ngo^{5} m^{4} zi^{1} dim^{2} • gaai^{2}.
   我 唔 知 點 解 。
   I don't know why.
   我不知道为什么。

4.3.6 A series of events : *(Track 090)*

To describe a series of events, use the following pattern:
event 1 + sin^{1} 先 *(first)* + gan^{1} • zyu^{6} 跟住 *(and then)* + event 2 …

P xiān… jiēzhe…
先…接着…

Examples:

1. Ngo^{5} sik^{6} • je^{5} sin^{1}, gan^{1} • zyu^{6} tai^{2} • syu^{1}, soeng^{5} • mong^{5}, fan^{3} • gaau^{3}.
   我 食 嘢 先 ， 跟 住 睇 書 、 上 網 、 瞓 覺 。
   I 'll grab something to eat first, then do some reading, surf the net and go to bed.
   我先吃东西，接着看书、上网、睡觉。

2. Ngo^{5} heoi^{3} lo^{2} cin^{2*} sin^{1}, gan^{1} • zyu^{6} heoi^{3} haang^{4} gaai^{1}, tai^{2} hei^{3}, sik^{6} faan^{6}.
   我 去 攞 錢 先 ， 跟 住 去 行 街 、 睇 戲 、 食 飯 。
   I'll withdraw some money first, then go shopping, watch a movie and have dinner.
   我先取钱，接着逛街、看电影、吃饭。

4.3.7 Word order (1) : *(Track 091)*

The basic word order in Cantonese is the same as that of English: subject-verb-object, as in "ngo^{5} 我 *(I)* zung^{1}• ji^{3} 鍾意 *(like / love)* nei^{5} 你 *(you)*" *(I love you)*.

However, when more information is added, the word order becomes quite different from that of English. Let's see how information such as 'with someone', 'specific time' or 'location of action' should be properly placed in Cantonese.

subject- verb- object
subject- with someone- verb- object
subject- with someone- specific time- verb- object
subject- with someone- specific time- location- verb- object

Examples:

1. Keoi^{5} tung^{4} ngo^{5} kam^{4} • jat^{6} heoi^{3} Wong^{6} • gok^{3} maai^{5} • je^{5}.
   佢 同 我 琴 日 去 旺 角 買 嘢 。
   She went with me to Mongkok and shopped around yesterday.
   她和我昨天去旺角买东西。

2. Lai^{5} • baai^{3} • luk^{6} ngo^{5} tung^{4} pang^{4} • jau^{5} hai^{2} Waan^{1} • zai^{2} tiu^{3} • mou^{5}.
禮 拜 六 我 同 朋 友 喺 灣 仔 跳 舞 。
I danced with my friend in Wanchai on Saturday.
礼 拜 六 我 和 朋 友 在 湾 仔 跳 舞 。

†† "*Time*" can be highlighted by placing it front of the subject as in example 2 .

4.4 Similar-sounding finals :

Some finals in Cantonese may sound alike for Putonghua and English speaking learners. In this section, we will focus on four similar-sounding pairs.

Please pay attention to the minimal pairs and listen carefully. Then mimic the words with similar finals.

(a) **ai - ei** *(Track 092)*

1.	gai^{1}	雞	chicken	gei^{1}	機	machine
2.	sai^{3}	細	small	sei^{3}	四	four

(b) **o - ou** *(Track 093)*

1.	go^{1}	歌	song	gou^{1}	高	tall
2.	do^{1}	多	many	dou^{1}	都	also

(c) **oi - eoi** *(Track 094)*

1.	zoi^{3}	再	again	zeoi^{3}	最	most
2.	goi^{2}	改	correct	geoi^{2}	舉	raise

(d) **in - ing** *(Track 095)*

1.	zin^{1}	煎	pan-fry	zing^{1}	蒸	steam
2.	sin^{1}	先	first	sing^{1}	星	star

4.5 Supplementary Vocabulary

4.5.1 Days of the week *(Track 096)*

No.	Cantonese Romanization	Chinese	Putonghua Romanization	Common spellings used in Hong Kong
1.	lai^{5} • baai^{3} • jat^{1}	禮拜一	lǐbài yī 礼拜一	Monday
2.	lai^{5} • baai^{3} • ji^{6}	禮拜二	lǐbài èr 礼拜二	Tuesday
3.	lai^{5} • baai^{3} • saam^{1}	禮拜三	lǐbài sān 礼拜三	Wednesday
4.	lai^{5} • baai^{3} • sei^{3}	禮拜四	lǐbài sì 礼拜四	Thursday
5.	lai^{5} • baai^{3} • ng^{5}	禮拜五	lǐbài wǔ 礼拜五	Friday
6.	lai^{5} • baai^{3} • luk^{6}	禮拜六	lǐbài liù 礼拜六	Saturday
7.	lai^{5} • baai^{3} • jat^{6}	禮拜日	lǐbài rì 礼拜日	Sunday

4.5.2 School facilities *(Track 097)*

No.	Cantonese Romanization	Chinese	Putonghua & Chinese Characters	Common spellings used in Hong Kong
1.	laam^{4} • kau^{4} • coeng^{4}	籃球場	lánqiú chǎng 篮球场	basketball court
2.	syu^{1} • guk^{2*}	書局	shūdiàn 书店	bookstore
3.	faan^{6} • tong^{4}	飯堂	shítáng 食堂	canteen
4.	fo^{3} • sat^{1}	課室	jiàoshì 教室	classroom
5.	sat^{6} • jim^{6} • sat^{1}	實驗室	shíyànshì 实验室	laboratory
6.	cyu^{5} • mat^{6} • gwai^{6}	儲物櫃	chǔwùguì 储物柜	locker
7.	caan^{1} • teng^{1}	餐廳	cāntīng 餐厅	restaurant
8.	haau^{6} • baa^{1} • zaam^{6}	校巴站	xuéxiào chēzhàn 学校车站	school bus stop
9.	wing^{6} • ci^{4}	泳池	yóuyǒngchí 游泳池	swimming pool
10.	sai^{2} • sau^{2} • gaan^{1}	洗手間	xǐshǒujiān 洗手间	washroom

4.5.3 Meals *(Track 098)*

No.	Cantonese Romanization	Chinese	Putonghua Romanization	Common spellings used in Hong Kong
1.	zou^{2} • caan^{1}	早餐	zǎofàn 早饭	breakfast
2.	aan^{3}	晏	wǔfàn 午饭	lunch
3.	haa^{6} • ng^{5} • caa^{4}	下午茶	xiàwǔchá 下午茶	afternoon tea, high tea
4.	maan^{5} • faan^{6}	晚飯	wǎnfàn 晚饭	dinner
5.	siu^{1} • je^{2*}	宵夜	yèxiāo 夜宵	midnight snack

4.5.4 Daily activities *(Track 099)*

No.	Cantonese Romanization	Chinese	Putonghua and Chinese Characters	Common spellings used in Hong Kong
1.	caat^{3} • ngaa^{4}	刷牙	shuā yá 刷牙	brush teeth
2.	wun^{6} • saam^{1}	換衫	huàn yīfu 换衣服	change clothes
3.	faa^{3} • zong^{1}	化妝	huàzhuāng 化妆	put on makeup
4.	zou^{6} gung^{1} • fo^{3}	做功課	zuò zuòyè 做作业	do homework
5.	faan^{1} uk^{1} • kei^{2*}	返屋企	huí jiā 回家	go home
6.	faan^{1} • hok^{6}	返學	shàngxué 上学	go to school
7.	faan^{1} • gung^{1}	返工	shàngbān 上班	go to work
8.	soeng^{5} • mong^{5}	上網	shàng wǎng 上网	surf the net
9.	sai^{2} • min^{6}	洗面	xǐ liǎn 洗脸	wash face
10.	tai^{2} din^{6} • si^{6}	睇電視	kàn diànshì 看电视	watch TV

4.6 Exercise

4.6.1 Matching

1. hai^{2} deoi^{3}•min^{6} 喺對面	________	A.	go straight ahead
2. zyun^{3} zo^{2} 轉左	________	B.	turn right
3. hai^{2} cin^{4}•min^{6} 喺前面	________	C.	opposite of
4. zyun^{3} jau^{6} 轉右	________	D.	in front (down the road)
5. jat^{1}•zik^{6} haang^{4} 一直行	________	E.	turn left

4.6.2 Multiple choice

1. *What time will you go to Mongkok?*

   Nei^{5} 你 gei^{2} 幾 ____________ heoi^{3} 去 Wong^{6}•gok^{3} 旺角 aa^{3} 呀 ?

   A. jat^{6} 日　　B. dim^{2}•gaai^{2} 點解　　C. dim^{2} 點

2. *Which day of the week do you learn tennis?*

   Nei^{5} 你 lai^{5}•baai^{3} 禮拜 ____________ hok^{6} 學 mong^{5}•kau^{4} 網球 aa^{3} 呀 ?

   A. bin^{1} 邊　　B. gei^{2} 幾　　C. me^{1} 咩

3. *We'll go to the library first, and then have afternoon tea.*

   Ngo^{5}•dei^{6} 我哋 heoi^{3} 去 tou^{4}•syu^{1}•gun^{2} 圖書館 ________ , ________ sik^{6} 食 tea.

   A. sin^{1} 先 , gan^{1}•zyu^{6} 跟住　　B. gan^{1}•zyu^{6} 跟住 , sin^{1} 先　　C. dou^{1} 都 , gan^{1}•zyu^{6} 跟住

4. *Both Tim and I are American.*

   Tim ____________ ngo^{5} 我 dou^{1} 都 hai^{6} 係 Mei^{5}•gwok^{3}•jan^{4} 美國人 .

   A. tung^{4} 同　　B. gei^{2} 幾　　C. dou^{1} 都

5. *Why are you busy every day?*

   ____________nei^{5} 我 mui^{5}•jat^{6} 每日 dou1 都 gam^{3} 咁 mong^{4} 忙 aa^{3} 呀 ?

   A. gan^{1}•zyu^{6} 跟住　　B. dim^{2}•gaai^{2} 點解　　C. gei^{2}•do^{1} cin^{2} 幾多

4.6.3 Fill in the blanks

A.	din^{6} • nou^{5} zung^{1} • sam^{1} 電腦中心	B.	je^{6} • maan^{5} 夜晚
C.	mou^{5} tong^{4} 冇堂	D.	lai^{5} • baai^{3} • ng^{5} 禮拜五
E.	sik^{6} zou^{2} • caan^{1} 食早餐	F.	tung^{4} 同
G.	ziu^{1} • zou^{2} 朝早	H.	gan^{1} • zyu^{6} 跟住
I.	fan^{3} • gaau^{3} 瞓覺	J.	sik^{6} aan^{3} 食晏

1. I have morning classes Monday to Friday. I have to get up at 8:00 a.m. everyday.

3. After class, I eat lunch with my classmate.

4. I don't have afternoon classes. I will go to the computer center to do homework.

2. After getting up, I brush my teeth, wash face, get dressed, eat breakfast, and then go to school.

5. At night, after dinner, I will surf the net first, then take a bath and go to bed.

1. Ngo^{5} lai^{5} • baai^{3} • jat^{1} dou^{3} _____ ziu^{1} • zou^{2} dou^{1} jau^{5} tong^{4}, _____ dou^{1} jiu^{3} baat^{3} dim^{2} hei^{2} • san^{1}.

   我 禮 拜 一 到 _____ 朝 早 都 有 堂 ， _____ 都 要 八 點 起 身 。

2. Hei^{2} • san^{1} zi^{1} • hau^{6} (*after*), ngo^{5} caat^{3} • ngaa^{4}, sai^{2} • min^{6}, wun^{6} • saam^{1}, _____, _____ faan^{1} • hok^{6}.

   起 身 之 後 ， 我 刷 牙 、 洗 面 、 換 衫 、 _____ ， _____ 返 學 。

3. Lok^{6} • zo^{2} • tong^{4}, ngo^{5} wui^{5} _____ tung^{4} • hok^{6} _____ .

   落 咗 堂 ， 我 會 _____ 同 學 _____ 。

4. Aan^{3} • zau^{3} _____, ngo^{5} wui^{5} heoi^{3} _____ zou^{6} gung^{1} • fo^{3}.

   晏 晝 _____ ， 我 會 去 _____ 做 功 課 。

5. _____ sik^{6} • zo^{2} maan^{5} • faan^{6} zi^{1} • hau^{6}, ngo^{5} wui^{5} (*will*) soeng^{5} • mong^{5} sin^{1}, gan^{1} • zyu^{6} cung^{1} loeng^{4}, _____.

   _____ 食 咗 晚 飯 之 後 ， 我 會 上 網 先 ， 跟 住 沖 涼 、 _____ 。

5 Heong¹•gong² ge³ gaau¹•tung¹

香港嘅交通 *Transportation in Hong Kong*

Learning Tasks

- to urge someone to do something
- to invite someone to do something
- to ask the way
- to talk about transportation
- to make a suggestion
- to ask about time spent in traffic
- to order Cantonese cuisine
- to give a reason to leave early

Grammar Notes

- adjective '*faster*': faai³ di¹ 快啲
- hours and minutes: zung¹•tau⁴ 鐘頭, fan¹•zung¹ 分鐘
- five-minute segments
- continuous marker : gan² 緊
- '*why not*': bat¹•jyu⁴ 不如
- '*how long*' questions: gei³•noi⁶ 幾耐
- serial verbs

Sounds and Tones

- Cantonese difficult finals

Supplementary Vocabulary

- mode of transport
- family members
- people around me
- Cantonese cuisine

Exercise

- matching
- multiple choice
- sentence order

 5.1 Vocabulary *(Track 100)*

No.	Cantonese Romanization	Cantonese Characters	Putonghua & Chinese Characters	English
1.	sai^3 • mui^{2*}	細妹	mèimei 妹妹	younger sister
2.	saang^1 • jat^6	生日	shēngrì 生日	birthday
3.	dang^2	等	děng 等	wait
4.	gan^2	緊	zhèngzài 正在	V-ing
5.	a) faai^3	快	kuài 快	fast / quick
	b) faai^3 di^1	快啲	kuài diǎn 快点	faster / be quick!
	c) gei^2 faai^3	幾快	tǐng kuài 挺快	quite fast
6.	a) faan^1	返	huí 回	return
	b) faan^1 uk^1 • kei^2	返屋企	huí jiā 回家	go home
7.	zik^1 • haak^1	即刻	lìkè 立刻	immediately
8.	bat^1 • jyu^4	不如	bùrú 不如	why not
9.	jat^1 • cai^4	一齊	yìqǐ 一起	together
10.	a) hai^2… heoi^3…	喺…去…	cóng 从 … qù 去 …	go from…to…
	b) hai^2 Wong^6 • gok^3 heoi^3 Sai^1 • gung^3	喺旺角去西貢	cóng Wàngjiǎo qù Xīgòng 从旺角去西贡	from Mong Kok to Sai Kung / go from Mong Kok to Sai Kung
	c) hai^2… lei^4…	喺…嚟…	cóng… lái… 从…来…	come from … to…
	d) hai^2 Waan^1 • zai^2 lei^4 Saa^1 • tin^4	喺灣仔嚟沙田	cóng Wānzǎi lái Shātián 从湾仔来沙田	come from Wan Chai to Shatin
11.	a) hou^2 gaai^3 • siu^6	好介紹	hǎo jièshào 好介绍	recommendable
	b) jau^5 me^1 hou^2 gaai^3 • siu^6	有咩好介紹	yǒu shénme hǎo jièshào? 有什么好介绍	do you have any recommendation?
12.	a) hoi^2 • sin^1	海鮮	hǎixiān 海鲜	seafood
	b) ziu^1 • jim^4 haa^1	椒鹽蝦	jiāoyán xiā 椒盐虾	fried shrimps with salt and pepper

	c) goeng¹ • cung¹ haai⁵	薑蔥蟹	jiāng cōng pángxiè 姜葱螃蟹	fried crabs with ginger and spring onion sauce
13.	a) hou² leng³	好靚	hěn xīnxiān 很新鲜	very fresh / nice / beautiful
	b) hou² hou² • sik⁶	好好食	hěn hǎo chī 很好吃	very delicious
	c) hou² hou² • mei⁶	好好味	wèidào hěn hǎo 味道很好	delicious / tasty
14.	caau² • faan⁶	炒飯	chǎo fàn 炒饭	fried rice
15.	a) gang² • hai⁶	梗係	dāngrán 当然	of course
	b) gang² • hai⁶ hou² laa¹	梗係好啦	dāngrán hǎo 当然好	of course good
16.	a) gaau¹ • tung¹	交通	jiāotōng 交通	traffic
	b) gaau¹ • tung¹ hou² fong¹ • bin⁶	交通好方便	jiāotōng hěn fāngbiàn 交通很方便	the transportation is convenient
17.	a) daap³	搭	zuò 坐	take (a mode of transport)
	b) daap³ me¹ ce¹	搭咩車	zuò shénme chē 坐什么车	what (mode of transport) are you taking
	c) daap³ dei⁶ • tit³	搭地鐵	zuò dìtiě 坐地铁	take the MTR
	d) daap³ siu² • baa¹	搭小巴	zuò xiǎobā 坐小巴	take a mini bus
	e) daap³ baa¹ • si²*	搭巴士	zuò bāshì 坐巴士	take a bus
18.	a) caa¹ • m⁴ • do¹	差唔多	chàbùduō 差不多	almost
	b) jat¹ go³ zung¹ • tau⁴	個鐘頭	yí ge xiǎoshí 一个小时	one hour
19.	a) zyu⁶	住	zhù 住	live,stay
	b) nei⁵ zyu⁶ hai² bin¹ • dou⁶	你住喺邊度	zhùzài nǎli 住在哪里	where do you live
	c) zyu⁶ hai² Wan¹ • zai²	住喺灣仔	zhùzài Wānzǎi 住在湾仔	live in Wan Chai
20.	ai¹ • jaa⁴	哎吔	āiyà 哎呀	interjection (wow, ouch, oops)
21.	gau² dim² gau²	九點九	jiǔ diǎn sì shí wǔ fēn 九点四十五分	nine forty-five

5.2 After watching a movie, Ka-Man receives a call from her mom.

(Track 101)

Wai2, Gaa1 • man5, gam1 • jat6 hai6 nei5/sai3 • mui2* saang1 • jat6, ngo5 • dei6 dou1 dang2 • gan2 nei5. Faai3 di1 faan1 • lei4 aa3!
喂，嘉敏，今日係你細妹生日，我哋都等緊你。快啲返嚟呀！
Hi, Ka-Man. Today is your younger sister's birthday. We are all waiting for you. Come home soon.
喂！嘉敏，今天是你妹妹生日，我们都在等你。快点回来吧！

Hou2, ngo5 zik1 • haak1 faan1 • lei4 laak3.
好，我即刻返嚟嘞。
Okay, I'll be back soon.
好，我马上回来。

After the phone call, Ka-Man asks to leave early.

M4 • hou2 • ji3 • si3*, ngo5 jiu3 faan1 uk1 • kei2* sik6 • faan6, zau2 sin1 laa3.
唔好意思，我要返屋企食飯，走先喇。
I'm sorry, I have to go home for dinner, so I should go now.
不好意思，我要回家吃饭，先走了。

M4 • gan2 • jiu3.
唔緊要。
That's okay.
没关系。

After Ka-Man has left, Tai-Lung invites Wing-Sze to eat dinner together.

Gaa1 • man5 faan1 uk1 • kei2* sik6 faan6, ngo5 • dei6 bat1 • jyu4 (jat1 • cai4 sik6 maan5 • faan6 aa1.
嘉敏返屋企食飯，我哋(不如一齊)食晚飯吖。
Ka-Man's gone home for dinner. Why don't the rest of us eat dinner together?
嘉敏回家吃饭，我们不如一起吃晚饭吧。

Ngo5 • dei6 heoi3 Sai1 • gung3 sik6 hoi2 • sin1, hou2 m4 hou2 aa3?
我哋去西貢食海鮮，好唔好呀？
How about we go to Sai Kung to eat seafood?
我们去西贡吃海鲜，好吗？

Gang2 • hai6 hou2 laa1! Ngo5 • dei6 dim2 heoi3 aa3?
梗係好啦！我哋點去呀？
That's of course good! How shall we get there?
当然好了！我们怎么去？

Ngo[5] • dei[6] ho[2] • ji[5] daap[3] dei[6] • tit[3] tung[4] siu[2] • baa[1] heoi[3].
我 哋 可 以 搭 地 鐵 同 小 巴 去 。
We can take the MTR and then a mini bus.
我们可以坐地铁和小巴去。

Hai[2] Wong[6] • gok[3] heoi[3] Sai[1] • gung[3], jiu[3] gei[2] • noi[6] aa[3]?
喺 旺 角 去 西 貢 ， 要 幾 耐 呀 ？
How long does it take to go from Mong Kok to Sai Kung?
从旺角到西贡，要多久？

Caa[1] • m[4] • do[1] jat[1] go[3] zung[1] • tau[4].
差 唔 多 一 個 鐘 頭 。
Almost an hour.
差不多一个小时。

They arrived at Sai Kung and enter a seafood restaurant.

Jau[5] me[1] hou[2] gaai[3] • siu[6] aa[3]?
有 咩 好 介 紹 呀 ？
Any good suggestions?
有什么好介绍？

Gam[1] • jat[6] ge[3] haa[1] tung[4] haai[5] dou[1] hou[2] leng[3] aa[3].
今 日 嘅 蝦 同 蟹 都 好 靚 呀 。
Today's shrimps and crabs are all very fresh.
今天的虾和螃蟹都很新鲜。

Gam[2], jiu[3] jat[1] go[3] ziu[1] • jim[4] haa[1] laa[1].
噉 ， 要 一 個 椒 鹽 蝦 啦 。
Then, we'll have a plate of deep-fried shrimps with salt & pepper.
那，来一个椒盐虾吧。

Ngo[5] jiu[3] goeng[1] • cung[1] haai[5] tung[4] caau[2] • faan[6].
我 要 薑 葱 蟹 同 炒 飯 。
I'd like to have a plate of crabs with ginger & spring onion sauce together with fried rice.
我要姜葱螃蟹和炒饭。

They talk about the traffic in Hong Kong.

Hai[2] Wong[6] • gok[3] lei[4] Sai[1] • gung[3] gei[2] faai[3] wo[3].
喺 旺 角 嚟 西 貢 幾 快 喎 。
It was pretty fast to come from Mong Kok to Sai Kung.
从旺角来西贡挺快的。

Hai6 aa3, Hoeng1 • gong2 ge3 gaau1 • tung1 hou2 fong1 • bin6.
係 呀 ， 香 港 嘅 交 通 好 方 便 。
That's right. It's easy to get around in Hong Kong.
对，香港的交通很方便。

Nei5 zyu6 hai2 bin1 • dou6 aa3?
你 住 喺 邊 度 呀 ？
Where do you live?
你住在哪里？

Ngo5 zyu6 hai2 Waan1 • zai2.
我 住 喺 灣 仔 。
I live in Wan Chai.
我住在湾仔。

Nei5 mui5 • jat6 daap3 me1 ce1 faan1 • hok6 aa3?
你 每 日 搭 咩 車 返 學 呀 ？
How do you get to school everyday?
你每天坐什么车上学？

Ngo5 daap3 baa1 • si2*. Nei5 zyu6 hai2 suk1 • se3 faan1 • hok6 zau6 fong1 • bin6 laa1.
我 搭 巴 士 。 你 住 喺 宿 舍 返 學 就 方 便 啦 。
I take a bus. You live in the dormitory, so going to school is convenient.
我坐公交车。你住在宿舍上学就方便了。

Hai6 aa3, ngo5 haang4 • lou6 zau6 dak1 laa3.
係 呀 ， 我 行 路 就 得 喇 。
Right, I can walk to school.
对呀，我走路就行了。

After the meal

Di1 hoi2 • sin1 tung4 caau2 • faan6 dou1 hou2 hou2 • sik6 aa3!
啲 海 鮮 同 炒 飯 都 好 好 食 呀 ！
The seafood and fried rice taste so nice.
这些海鲜和炒饭很好吃！

Hai6 aa3, zan1 • hai6 hou2 hou2 • mei6 aa3.
係 呀 ， 真 係 好 好 味 呀 。
Yes, they're really delicious.
對，味道真好。

Ai1 • jaa3! Ji5 • ging1 gau2 dim2 gau2, ngo5 ting1 • jat6 ziu1 • zou2 gau2 dim2 jau5 tong4, jiu3 zau2 laa3.
哎 吔 ！ 已 經 九 點 九 ， 我 聽 日 朝 早 九 點 有 堂 ， 要 走 啦 。
Look, it's already nine forty-five. I have class at nine tomorrow morning. I'd better be off now.
哎呀！已经九点四十五分了，我明天早上九点有课，该走了。

Gam2, jat1 • cai4 zau2 laa1!
噉 ， 一 齊 走 啦 ！
Then let's leave together.
那么，我们一起走吧！

5.3 Grammar Notes

5.3.1 Adjective *'faster'* : faai3 di1 快啲 *(Track 102)*

To urge someone to do something, "faai3 di1 快啲 *(hurry up / faster)*" is used before a verb phrase.

P kuàidiǎnr
快点儿

Examples:

1. Faai3 di1 haang4 laa1.
   快 啲 行 啦 。
   Walk faster / Hurry up and go.
   快点走吧。

2. Nei5 gon2 si4 • gaan3, faai3 di1 sik6 laa1.
   你 趕 時 間 ， 快 啲 食 啦 。
   You're in a hurry, hurry up and eat.
   你赶时间，快点吃吧。

5.3.2 Hours & minutes : zung1 • tau4 鐘頭, fan1 • zung1 分鐘 *(Track 103)*

To ask the number of hours spent, "gei2 • do1 幾多 *(how many)* + go3 個 *(classifier)* + jung1 • tau4 鐘頭 *(hour)*" is put after the verb (and before the object if there is). Likewise, the number of minutes spent can be asked with "gei2 • do1 幾多 *(how many)* + fan1 • zung1 分鐘 *(minute)*".

P xiǎoshí 小时
fēnzhōng 分钟

Examples:

1. *Q:* Nei^5 mui^5 • jat^6 tai^2 gei^2 • do^1 go^3 zung^1 • tau^4 din^6 • si^6 aa^3?
   你 每 日 睇 幾 多 個 鐘 頭 電 視 呀 ？
   How many hours do you watch TV every day?
   你每天看几个小时电视？

   A: Ngo^5 mui^5 • jat^6 tai^2 saam^1 go^3 zung^1 • tau^4.
   我 每 日 睇 三 個 鐘 頭 。
   I watch three hours every day.
   我每天看三个小时。

2. *Q:* Gung^1 • zai^2 • min^6 jiu^3 zyu^2 gei^2 • do^1 fan^1 • zung^1 aa^3?
   公 仔 麵 要 煮 幾 多 分 鐘 呀 ？
   How many minutes do you need to cook instant noodles?
   方便面要煮几分钟啊？

   A: Jiu^3 zyu^2 ng^5 fan^1 • zung^1.
   要 煮 五 分 鐘 。
   You should cook for five minutes.
   要煮五分钟。

5.3.3 Five minute segments : *(Track 104)*

Since each numberal on a clock denotes a five-minute segment, "jat^1 • go^3 • zi^6 一個字" means '*five minutes*' in Cantonese. "Jat^1 • go^3 • zi^6 一個字" is also used to refer to the clock time when a long hand is on the one, thus '*five past*'. '*Five past*' is also expressed with "daap^6 • jat^1 搭一" or simply " jat^1 一" after "X + dim^2 點". You can guess what other numbers refer to except that '*half an hour*' is called "bun^3 go^3 zung^1 • tau^4 半個鐘頭", and '*X o' clock sharp*' is expressed with "daap^6 zeng^3 X + dim^2 搭正X點" or "X dim^2 zing^3 X點正" as shown below.

Common clock time expressions:

C		P
sap^6 dim^2 saam^3	十點三	十点一刻
sap^6 dim^2 daap^6 • saam^3	十點搭三	
sap^6 dim^2 saam^3 • go^3 • zi^6	十點三個字	
luk^6 dim^2 gau^2	六點九	六点三刻
luk^6 dim^2 daap^6 • gau^2	六點搭九	
luk^6 dim^2 gau^2 • go^3 • zi^6	六點九個字	

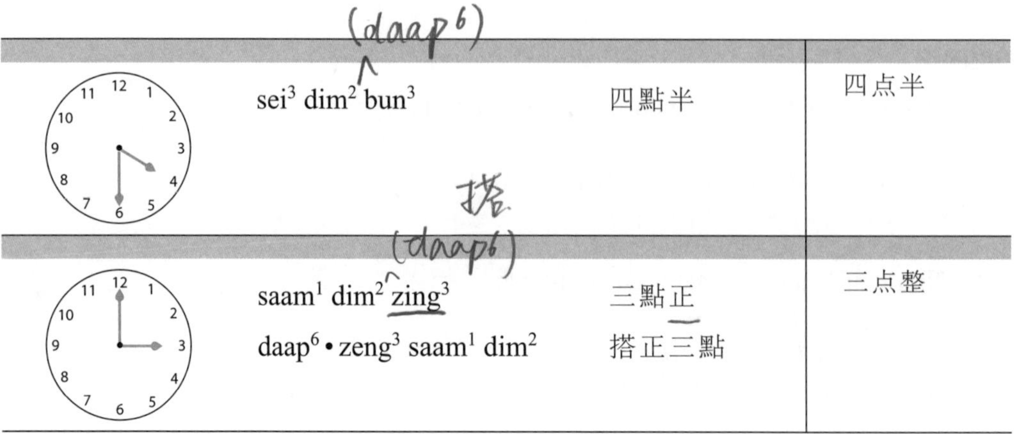

(clock)	sei^{3} dim^{2} bun^{3}	四點半	四点半
(clock)	saam^{1} dim^{2} zing^{3} daap^{6} • zeng^{3} saam^{1} dim^{2}	三點正 搭正三點	三点整

Examples:

1. *Q:* Ji^{4} • gaa^{1} gei^{2} dim^{2} aa^{3}?
   而 家 幾 點 呀 ？
   What time is it now?
   现 在 几 点 ？

   A: Ji^{4} • gaa^{1} loeng^{5} dim^{2} baat^{3}.
   而 家 兩 點 八 。
   It's two twenty now.
   现 在 两 点 四 十 分 。

2. *Q:* Nei^{5} gei^{2} dim^{2} soeng^{5} • tong^{4} aa^{3}?
   你 幾 點 上 堂 呀 ？
   What time do you have class?
   你 几 点 上 课 ？

   A: Ngo^{5} sap^{6} dim^{2} bun^{3} soeng^{5} • tong^{4}.
   我 十 點 半 上 堂 。
   I have class at half past ten.
   我 十 点 半 上 课 。

5.3.4 Continuous marker : gan^{2} 緊 *(Track 105)*

"V-gan^{2} 緊" is similar to English '*V-ing*', showing an on-going action. Note that "gan^{2} 緊" is placed between the verb and the object, e.g. is expressed "sik^{6} • gan^{2} faan^{6} 食緊飯 *(eating)*".

P zhèngzài
正在，在

Examples:

1. Nei^{5} zou^{6} • gan^{2} me^{1} aa^{3}?
   你 做 緊 咩 呀 ？
   What are you doing?
   你 在 干 嘛 ？

2. Ngo[5] soeng[5] • gan[2] • mong[5].
我 上 緊 網 。
I am surfing the Net.
我在上网。

5.3.5 '*Why not*': bat[1] • jyu[4] 不如 + suggestion (Track 106)

"Bat[1] • jyu[4] 不如" is used in front of the main verb or sentence when giving someone a suggestion. You can also use it when introducing a new topic, as in "Bat[1] • jyu[4] gong[2] • haa[5] heoi[3] bin[1] • dou[6] waan[2] 不如講吓去邊度玩 *(Why don't we talk about where to go for fun)*", etc.

P bùrú 不如

Examples:

1. Dang[2] • zo[2] gam[3] noi[6] dou[1] mou[5] baa[1] • si[2]*, bat[1] • jyu[4] daap[3] dik[1] • si[2]* laa[1].
等 咗 咁 耐 都 冇 巴 士 ， 不 如 搭 的 士 啦 。
We've waited so long, but no bus has come. Why don't we take a taxi?
等了这么久都没有公交车，不如打的吧。

2. Hou[2] hou[2] • sik[6] aa[3], bat[1] • jyu[4] giu[3] do[1] di[1] laa[1].
好 好 食 呀 ， 不 如 叫 多 啲 啦 。
They taste so good. Why don't we order some more?
很好吃，不如多叫一些吧。

5.3.6 '*How long*' questions: gei[3] • noi[6] 幾耐 (Track 107)

To ask the travel time from place 1 to place 2, the following pattern is used: "hai[2] 喺 *(from)* + place 1 + heoi[3] 去 *(go)* / lei[4] 嚟 *(come)* + place 2 + jiu[3] 要 *(go)* + gei[2] • noi[6] 幾耐 *(how long)*".

P cóng … qù / lái … yào duō jiǔ 从…去 / 来… 要多久

Examples:

1. Hai[2] Wong[6] • gok[3] heoi[3] Zim[1] • saa[1] • zeoi[2] jiu[3] gei[2] noi[6] aa[3]?
喺 旺 角 去 尖 沙 咀 要 幾 耐 呀 ？
How long does it take from Mong Kok to Tsim Sha Tsui?
从旺角去尖沙咀要多久？

2. Saam[1] - sei[3] • go[3] • zi[6] laa[1].
三 四 個 字 啦 。
Fifteen to twenty minutes.
十五到二十分钟吧。

5.3.7 Serial verbs : *(Track 108)*

A series of actions such as taking the transport to go somewhere and do something, can be expressed in the following way:

P zuò … qù
坐…去

Subject + **daap³ 搭** (*take*) + transportation + **heoi³ 去** (*go*) + destination + Verb phrase

Examples:

1. *A:* Nei⁵ • dei⁶ daap³ me¹ ce¹ heoi³ hei³ • jyun²* tai² • hei³ aa³?
   你 哋 搭 咩 車 去 戲 院 睇 戲 呀 ？
   What (mode of transport) are you taking to go to the cinema to watch the movie?
   你们坐什么车去电影院看电影？

   B: Daap³ baa¹ • si²*.
   搭 巴 士 。
   Take the bus.
   坐公交。

2. Keoi⁵ daap³ syun⁴ heoi³ Ou³ • mun²* sik⁶ Pou⁴ • gwok³ • coi³.
   佢 搭 船 去 澳 門 食 葡 國 菜 。
   He takes a ferry to go to Macau to eat Portuguese food.
   他坐船去澳门吃葡萄牙菜。

5.4 Cantonese difficult finals :

Cantonese has "oe" & "eo" finals ythat are missing in Putonghua & English . The "oe" only carry "ng", "k" endings, while "eo" only carry "n" ,"i" and "t" endings.

Listen carefully and mimic the following words.

(a) oe : a long vowel similar to "er" in 'her' in British English with round lips *(Track 109)*

1. doe²	朵	cluster of flowers	2. hoe¹	靴	boots

(b) oeng : a long vowel "oe" followed by "-ng" *(Track 110)*

1. coeng³	唱	sing	2. loeng⁵	兩	two

(c) oek : a long vowel "oe" followed by "-k" *(Track 111)*

1. goek³	腳	feet	2. joek⁶	藥	medicine

(d) eoi : a short vowel with semi-open rounded lips, followed by "-i" *(Track 112)*

1. deoi³	對	pair	2. seoi²	水	water

(e) eon : a short vowel "eo' followed by "-n" *(Track 113)*

1.	ceon^{2}	蠢	stupid	2.	seon^{3}	信	believe

(f) eot : a short vowel "eo" followed by "-t" *(Track 114)*

1.	ceot^{1}	出	out	2.	seot^{6}	術	skill

5.5 Supplementary Vocabulary

5.5.1 Mode of transport *(Track 115)*

No.	Cantonese Romanization	Chinese	Putonghua and Chinese Characters	English
1.	fei^{1} • gei^{1}	飛機	fēijī 飞机	airplane
2.	daan^{1} • ce^{1}	單車	zìxíngchē 自行车	bicycle
3.	baa^{1} • si^{2}*	巴士	gōngjiāo 公交 / bāshì 巴士	bus
4.	syun^{4}	船	chuán 船	ferry / ship
5.	siu^{2} • baa^{1}	小巴	xiǎo bāshì 小巴士	mini bus
6.	dei^{6} • tit^{3}	地鐵	dìtiě 地铁	MTR
7.	saan^{1} • deng^{2} laam^{6} • ce^{1}	山頂纜車	shāndǐng lǎnchē 山顶缆车	peak tram
8.	dik^{1} • si^{2}*	的士	chūzū chē 出租车	taxi
9.	fo^{2} • ce^{1}	火車	huǒchē 火车	train
10.	din^{6} • ce^{1} / ding^{1} • ding^{1}	電車 / 叮叮	diànchē 电车	tram

5.5.2 People around me *(Track 116)*

No.	Cantonese Romanization	Chinese	Putonghua and Chinese Characters	English
1.	naam^{4} pang^{4} • jau^{5}	男朋友	nán péngyou 男朋友	boyfriend
2.	tung^{4} • si^{6}	同事	tóngshì 同事	colleague
3.	pang^{4} • jau^{5}	朋友	péngyou 朋友	friend
4.	neoi^{5} pang^{4} • jau^{5}	女朋友	nǚ péngyou 女朋友	girlfriend
5.	leon^{4} • geoi^{1}	鄰居	línoū 邻居	labour
6.	jip^{6} • zyu^{2}	業主	fángdōng 房东	landlord

7.	can^{1} • cik^{1}	親戚	qīnqi 亲戚	relative
8.	tung^{4} • fong^{2*}	同房	tóngwū 同屋 / shìyǒu 室友	roommate / housemate
9.	dou^{6} • si^{1}	導師	dǎoshī 导师	supervisor
10.	lou^{5} • si^{1}	老師	lǎoshī 老师	teacher

5.5.3 Family members *(Track 117)*

†† The Chinese kinship term system is complicated. Terms to address relatives on father's side (same surname) differ from those on mother's side (different surname). Note that Cantonese kinship terms are often different from those in Putonghua.

5.5.4 Cantonese Cuisine *(Track 118)*

No.	Cantonese Romanization	Chinese	Putonghua Romanization	English
1.	jyu^4 • hoeng^1 ke^2 • zi^2	魚香茄子	yú xiāng qiézi 鱼香茄子	braised eggplant with minced pork
2.	Zung^1 • sik^1 ngau^4 • lau^5	中式牛柳	zhōngshì niúliǔ 中式牛柳	Chinese-style beef steak with sweet & sour sauce
3.	pei^4 • paa^4 dau^6 • fu^6	琵琶豆腐	pípá dòufu 琵琶豆腐	deep-fried tofu with minced fish
4.	maa^4 • po^4 dau^6 • fu^6	麻婆豆腐	mápó dòufu 麻婆豆腐	Mapo tofu, tofu with minced meat in chili-sauce
5.	siu^1 aap^{2*}	燒鴨	shāo yā 烧鸭	roast goose
6.	si^6 • jau^4 gai^1	豉油雞	chǐyóu jī 豉油鸡	soya sauce chicken
7.	cing^1 • zing^1 sek^6 • baan^1	清蒸石斑	qīngzhēng shíbān 清蒸石斑	steamed grouper
8.	syun^3 • jung^4 caau^2 coi^3 • sam^1	蒜蓉炒菜心	suàn róng chǎo cài xīn 蒜蓉炒菜心	stir-fried Chinese cabbage with garlic
9.	sai^1 • laan^4 • faa^1 caau^2 daai^3 • zi^2	西蘭花炒帶子	xīlánhuā chǎo dàizi (bèizi) 西兰花炒带子（鲜贝）	stir-fried scallop with broccoli
10.	baak^6 • coek^3 haa^1	白灼蝦	bái zhuóxiā 白灼虾	white boiled shrimp

5.6 Exercise

5.6.1 Matching

1. gang^2 • hai^6 梗係 ___D___
2. gan^2 緊 ___E___
3. faan^1 uk^1 • kei^{2*} 返屋企 ___A___
4. hou^2 leng^3 好靚 ___C___
5. m^4 • gan^2 • jiu^3 唔緊要 ___B___

A. go home
B. not important
C. very fresh / pretty
D. of course
E. continuous action

5.6.2 Multiple choice

1. *I have been waiting for half an hour.*

   Ngo^5 我 dang^2 • zo^2 等咗 __________ 。

   A. bun^3 go^3 zung^1 • tau^4 半個鐘頭　　B. bun^3 zung^1 • tau^4 半鐘頭　　C. bun^3 go^3 fan^1 • zung^1 半個分鐘

2. *It's seven thirty-five now.*

   Ji^4 • gaa^1 而家 cat^1 七 dim^2 點 __________ 。

   A. ng^5 五　　B. saam^1 三　　C. cat^1 七

3. *I want to learn faster.*

   Ngo^5 我 soeng^2 想 hok^6 學 __________ 。

   A. hou^2 faai^3 好快　　B. faai^3 di^1 快啲　　C. faai^3 dei^6 快哋

4. *How long does it take to go from Central to Sha Tin?*

   __________ Zung^1 • waan^4 中環 heoi^3 去 Saa^1 • tin^4 沙田 jiu^3 要 gei^2 • noi^6 幾耐 aa^3 呀？

   A. zoi^6 在　　B. hai^6 係　　C. hai^2 喺

5. *I take the MTR and a minibus to go to Sai Kung to eat seafood.*

   Ngo^5 我 daap 搭 __________ tung^4 同 __________ heoi^3 去 Sai^1 • gung^3 西貢 sik^6 食 hoi^2 • sin^1 海鮮。

   A. fo^2 • ce^1 火車，dei^6 • tit^1 地鐵　　B. dei^6 • tit^1 地鐵，siu^2 • baa^2 小巴　　C. siu^2 • baa^1 小巴，fo^2 • ce^1 火車

5.6.3 Sentence order

Rearrange the words in the correct order as shown in the example.

Example :

I'll go to Sha Tin with my classmate.

heoi^3 去	tung^4 • hok^6 同學	Saa^1 • tin^4 沙田	tung^4 同	ngo^5 我
(4)	(3)	(5)	(2)	(1)

1. ge3 嘅　fong1 • bin6 方便　Hoeng1 • gong2 香港　hou2 好　gaau1 • tung1 交通

　(2)　(5)　(1)　(4)　(3)

2. lei4 嚟　uk1 • kei2* 屋企　hok6 • haau6 學校　hai2 喺　jiu3 saam1 • go3 • zi6 要三個字

　(3)　(4)　(2)　(1)　(5)

3. ngo5 我　saang1 • jat6 生日　hai6 係　maa4 • maa1 媽媽　gam1 • jat6 今日

　(3)　(5)　(2)　(4)　(1)

4. tung4 同　ngo5 我　tai2 • syu1 睇書　pang4 • jau5 朋友　heoi3 tou4 • syu1 • gun2 去圖書館

　(2)　(1)　(5)　(3)　(4)

5. heoi3 去　ngo5 • dei6 我哋　bat1 • jyu4 不如　aa1 吖　jam2 be1 • zau2 飲啤酒

　(3)　(1)　(2)　(5)　(4)

6

Daa^2 din^6 • waa^{2*}

打 電 話 *Making phone calls*

Learning Tasks

- to ask for & give a phone number
- to talk with someone on the phone
- to respond to an apology
- to ask & indicate availability
- to talk about a purpose
- to talk about an appointment
- to indicate a place to meet

Language Focus

- adjective '*important*': gan^2 • jiu^3 緊要
- '(*give a phone call*) *to*...': bei^2 俾
- verb '*look for*': wan^2 搵
- '(*someone*) *is in*': hai^2 • dou^6 喺度
- '*when*' questions: gei^2 • si^4 幾時
- '*meet someone at some place*': hai^2 喺 + place + dang^2 等 + person
- verb suffix '*back*': faan^1 返

Sounds and Tones

- Cantonese tones

Supplementary Vocabulary

- looking for someone on the phone
- answering the phone
- dates
- MTR stations in Hong Kong

Exercise

- matching
- multiple choice
- sentence order

6.1 Vocabulary *(Track 119)*

No.	Cantonese Romanization	Cantonese Characters	Putonghua & Chinese Characters	English
1.	aa^{4}	嗱	ma 吗	final particle for conformation
2.	daa^{2} • co^{3}	打錯	dăcuò 打错	wrong number
3.	mou^{5} ni^{1} go^{3} jan^{4}	冇呢個人	méiyǒu zhège rén 没有这个人	no such person
4.	a) m^{4} • gan^{2} • jiu^{3}	唔緊要	búyàojǐn 不要紧	never mind
	b) gan^{2} • jiu^{3} si^{6}	緊要事	yàojǐn de shì 要紧的事	important matter
5.	gwai^{3} sing^{3}	貴姓	guìxìng 贵姓	may I have your surname
6.	wan^{2}	搵	zhǎo 找	find
7.	Can^{4} siu^{2} • ze^{2}	陳小姐	Chén xiǎojie 陈小姐	Miss Chan
8.	Lei^{5} saang^{1}	李生	Lǐ xiānsheng 李先生	Mr. Lee / Li
9.	a) daa^{2} din^{6} • waa^{2*}	打電話	dǎ diànhuà 打电话	make a phone call
	b) daa^{2} • faan^{1} din^{6} • waa^{2*} bei^{2} ngo^{5}	打返電話俾我	gěi wǒ huí diànhuà 给我回电话	call back
	c) ceng^{2} keoi^{5} daa^{2} • faan^{1} din^{6} • waa^{2*} bei^{2} ngo^{5}	請佢打返電話俾我	qǐng tā gěi wǒ huí diànhuà 请他给我回电话	ask him / her to call back
	d) daa^{2} • zo^{2} gei^{2} ci^{3} din^{6} • waa^{2*} bei^{2} nei^{5}	打咗幾次電話俾你	gěi nǐ dǎle jǐ cì diànhuà 给你打了几次电话	I've called you several times
10.	din^{6} • waa^{2*} hou^{6} • maa^{5}	電話號碼	diànhuà hàomă 电话号码	phone number
11.	teng^{1} • gong^{2}	聽講	tīngshuō 听说	I heard
12.	ni^{1} paai^{2*}	呢排	zuìjìn 最近	recently
13.	hoi^{1} • zo^{2}	開咗	kāile 开了	opened
14.	a) jat^{1} gaan^{1}	一間	yì jiā 一家 / yì suǒ 一所	classifier for buildings
	b) jat^{1} gaan^{1} sing^{1} • kap^{1} ge^{3} ping^{4} • man^{4} dim^{2} • sam^{1} zyun^{1} • mun^{4} • dim^{3}	一間星級嘅平民點心專門店	yì jiā xīngjí píngmín de diǎnxīn zhuānméndiàn 一家星级平民的点心专门店	a star-rated dimsum restaurant

15.	a) soeng^{2}	想	xiǎng 想	want to
	b) m^{4} soeng^{2}	唔想	bùxiǎng 不想	don't want to
	c) soeng^{2} m^{4} soeng^{2} si^{3} • haa^{5} aa^{3}	想唔想試吓呀	yào bu yào shìshi 要不要试试	would you like to give it a try
16.	a) aak^{3}	呃	de 的	sentence particle to show finality
	b) hou^{2} aak^{3}	好呃	hǎo de 好的	Sure (expressing agreement)
17.	a) gei^{2} • si^{4}	幾時	shénme shíhou 什么时候	when
	b) gei^{2} • si^{4} dak^{1} • haan^{4}	幾時得閒	shénme shíhou yǒu kòng? 什么时候有空？	when are you free?
18.	hau^{6} • jat^{6}	後日	hòutiān 后天	the day after tomorrow
19.	a) dang^{2}	等	děng 等	wait
	b) hai^{2} bin^{1} • dou^{6} dang^{2}	喺邊度等	zài nǎr děng 在哪儿等	where shall we meet
	c) hai^{2} Zim^{1} • saa^{1} • zeoi^{2} dang^{2}	喺尖沙咀等	zài Jiānshāzuǐ děng 在尖沙咀等	meet at Tsim Sha Tsui
	d) hai^{2} Zim^{1} • saa^{1} • zeoi^{2} dei^{6} • tit^{3} zaam^{6} dang^{2}	喺尖沙咀地鐵站等	zài Jiānshāzuǐ dìtiě zhàn děng 在尖沙咀地铁站等	meet at Tsim Sha Tsui MTR station
	e) hai^{2} Zim^{1} • saa^{1} • zeoi^{2} dei^{6} • tit^{3} zaam^{6} Hang^{4} • sang^{1} ngan^{4} • hong^{4} dang^{2}	喺尖沙咀地鐵站恒生銀行等	zài Jiānshāzuǐ dìtiě zhàn Héngshēng yínháng děng 在尖沙咀地铁站恒生银行等	meet at the Hang Seng Bank at Tsim Sha Tsui MTR station
	f) hai^{2} Zim^{1} • saa^{1} • zeoi^{2} dei^{6} • tit^{3} zaam^{6} Hang^{4} • sang^{1} ngan^{4} • hong^{4} cin^{4} • min^{6} dang^{2}	喺尖沙咀地鐵站恒生銀行前面等	zài Jiānshāzuǐ dìtiě zhàn Héngshēng yínháng qián-mian děng 在尖沙咀地铁站恒生银行前面等	meet in front of the Hang Seng Bank at Tsim Sha Tsui MTR station
20.	do^{1} di^{1} jan^{4}	多啲人	gèng duō de rén 更多的人	more people
21.	sik^{6} dim^{2} • sam^{1}	食點心	chī diǎnxīn 吃点心	eat dim sum
22.	hoi^{1} • sam^{1}	開心	gāoxìng 高兴	happy

23.	a) zung^{6}	仲	hái 还	still
	b) zung^{6} soeng^{2}	仲想	hái xiǎng 还想	still want to
	c) zung^{6} soeng^{2} joek^{3} bin^{1} • go^{3}	仲想約邊個	hái xiǎng yuē shéi 还想约谁	who else do you want to invite
24.	baai^{1} • baai^{3}	拜拜	zàijiàn 再见	good-bye
25.	hai^{2} Zim^{1} • dei^{6} • Hang^{4} gin^{3}	喺尖地恒見	zài Jiān(shāzuǐ) dì(tiě zhàn) Héng(shēng yínháng) jiàn 在尖（沙咀）地（铁站）恒（生银行）见	meet at Tsim Sha Tsui MTR station Hang Seng Bank* *abbreviation

6.2 Tai-Lung gives Ka-Man a phone call. *(Track 120)*

Wai^{2}, Gaa^{1} • man^{5} aa^{4}?
喂 ！ 嘉 敏 嗱 ？
Hello! Is that Ka-Man?
喂 ！ 是 嘉 敏 吗 ？

Nei^{5} daa^{2} • co^{3} laa^{3}, ni^{1} • dou^{6} mou^{5} ni^{1} go^{3} jan^{4}.
你 打 錯 喇 ， 呢 度 冇 呢 個 人 。
Wrong number, there is no such person here.
你 打 错 了 ， 这 里 没 有 这 个 人 。

O^{4}, m^{4} • hou^{2} • ji^{3} • si^{3}*.
哦 ， 唔 好 意 思 。
Oh, I'm sorry.
哦 ！ 不 好 意 思 。

M^{4} • gan^{2} • jiu^{3}.
唔 緊 要 。
Never mind.
没 关 系 。

Tai-Lung makes a call again

Ceng^{2} • man^{6} gwai^{3} sing^{3} wan^{2} Can^{4} siu^{2} • ze^{2}?
請 問 貴 姓 搵 陳 小 姐 ？
May I ask who is calling Miss Chan?
请 问 贵 姓 找 陈 小 姐 ？

Ngo^5 hai^6 Lei^5 Daai^6 • lung^4.
我 係 李 大 龍 。
This is Tai-Lung Lee.
我是李大龙。

Lei^5 saang^1, ceng^2 • man^6 jau^5 me^1 si^6 wan^2 Can^4 siu^2 • ze^2?
李 生 ， 請 問 有 咩 事 搵 陳 小 姐 ？
Mr. Lee, may I ask what you'd like to find her for?
李先生，请问有甚么事找陈小姐？

M^4 • goi^1 ceng^2 keoi^5 daa^2 • faan^1 din^6 • waa^{2*} bei^2 ngo^5.
唔 該 請 佢 打 返 電 話 俾 我 。
Would you please ask her to call me back?
请你请她给我回电话。

Hou^2 aak^3, nei^5 ge^3 din^6 • waa^2 hou^6 • maa^5, m^4 • goi^1.
好 呃 ， 你 嘅 電 話 號 碼 ， 唔 該 。
Certainly. Your number, please?
好的，请你说你的电话号码。

Luk^6 jat^1 ji^6 sei^3 baat^3 cat^1 saam^1 gau^2.
6 1 2 4 - 8 7 3 9 。
My number is 6124-8739.
我的电话号码是61248739。

Later Ka-Man calls Tai-Lung back.

Wai^2, Daai^6 • lung^4, nei^5 wan^2 ngo^5 aa^4?
喂 ， 大 龍 ， 你 搵 我 嗬 ？
Hi, Tai-Lung. Did you call me?
喂！大龙，你找我吗？

Hai^6 aa^3, ngo^5 daa^2 • zo^2 gei^2 ci^3 din^6 • waa^{2*} bei^2 nei^5.
係 呀 ， 我 打 咗 幾 次 電 話 俾 你 。
Yes, I called you several times.
对。我给你打了几次电话。

Wan^2 ngo^5 jau^5 me^1 gan^2 • jiu^3 si^6 aa^3?
搵 我 有 咩 緊 要 事 呀 ？
Did you call me for anything important?
找我有什么要紧的事吗？

Teng1 • gong2 ni1 • paai2* hoi1 • zo2 jat1 gaan1 sing1 • kap1 ge3 ping4 • man4 dim2 • sam1 zyun1 • mun4 • dim3, nei5 soeng2 m4 soeng2 heoi3 si3 • haa5?
聽講呢排開咗一間星級嘅平民點心專門店，你想唔想去試吓？
I heard that there is a newly-opened star-rated dimsum restaurant. Do you want to try it out?
听说最近开了一家星级平民的点心专门店，你要不要去试试？

Soeng2 aa3. Nei5 gei2 • si4 dak1 • haan4 aa3?
想呀。你幾時得閒呀？
Yes, I do. When will you be free?
要。你什么时候有空？

Ngo5 hau6 • jat6 dak1 • haan4, nei5 ne1?
我後日得閒，你呢？
I will be free the day after tomorrow. How about you?
我后天有空，你呢？

Ngo5 hau6 • jat6 dou1 dak1 • haan4.
我後日都得閒。
I will be free the day after tomorrow, too.
我后天也有空。

Gei2 dim2 aa3?
幾點呀？
What time?
几点？

Aan3 • zau3 jat1 dim2 laa1.
晏晝一點啦。
One o'clock in the afternoon.
下午一点吧。

Hou2 aak3, hai2 bin1 • dou6 dang2 aa3?
好呃，喺邊度等呀？
Sure. Where shall we meet?
好的，在哪里等。

Hai2 Zim1 • saa1 • zeoi2 dei6 • tit3 zaam6 Hang4 • sang1 ngan4 • hong4 cin4 • min6 dang2, dak1 m4 dak1 aa3?
喺尖沙咀地鐵站恒生銀行前面等，得唔得呀？
Could we meet at Tsim Sha Tsui MTR station, in front of the Hang Seng Bank?
在尖沙咀地铁站恒生银行前面等，好吗？

Dak[1]!
得 。
Okay.
行。

Do[1] di[1] jan[4] sik[6] dim[2] • sam[1] hoi[1] • sam[1] • di[1], nei[5] zung[6] soeng[2] joek[3] bin[1] • go[3] heoi[3] aa[3]?
多啲人食點心開心啲，你仲想約邊個去呀？
We'll have more fun if more people eat dimsum together. Who else would you like to invite?
多些人吃点心更高兴，你还想约谁去？

Wing[6] • si[1] tung[4] Gaa[3] • naam[4], hou[2] m[4] hou[2] aa[3]?
詠詩同家男，好不好呀？
Shall we invite Wing-Sze and Ka-Nam?
咏诗和家男，好吗？

Hou[2] aak[3].
好呃 。
Sure.
好的。

Gam[2], ngo[5] daa[2] din[6] • waa[2]* bei[2] Wing[6] • si[1], nei[5] daa[2] bei[2] Gaa[1] • naam[4] laa[1].
噉，我打電話俾詠詩，你打俾家男啦。
Then I'll call Wing-Sze and you could call Ka-Nam.
那么，我给咏诗打电话，你给家男打电话吧。

Hou[2] aak[3], hai[2] "Zim[1] • dei[6] • hang[4]" gin[3] laa[1].
好呃，喺「尖地恒」見啦。
No problem. See you at "Tsim" "M(TR)" "Hang".
好的，在「尖地恒」见啦。

6.3 Grammar Notes

6.3.1 Adjective '*important*' : gan[2] • jiu[3] 緊要 *(Track 121)*

The word to express '*important*' in Cantonese is "gan[2] • jiu[3] 緊要". It's interesting to note that the corresponding word of gan[2] • jiu[3] in Putonghua is similar but the word order is not the same.

P yàojǐn 要紧

Examples:

1. Ngo5 jau5 di1 gan2 • jiu1 si6, soeng2 zau2 sin1.
   我 有 啲 緊 要 事 ， 想 走 先 。
   As I have something important, I want to leave early.
   我有些要紧的事，想先走。

2. M4 • gan2 • jiu3, nei5 zau2 sin1 laa1.
   唔 緊 要 ， 你 走 先 啦 。
   Never mind, you can go ahead and leav first.
   没关系，你先走。

6.3.2 '(*Give a phone call*) *to…*' : bei2 俾 *(Track 122)*

In Cantonese, "to give a phone call to someone" is expressed by "daa2 din6 • waa2* 打电话 + bei2 俾 + *someone*" or "ko1 (call) + *someone*". Note that unlike Putonghua, the phone recipient must be expressed after the verb "daa2" .

P gěi 给 + *someone* + dǎ diànhuà 打电话

Examples:

1. Nei5 dak1 • haan4 daa2 din6 • waa2* bei2 ngo5 aa1.
   你 得 閒 打 電 話 俾 我 吖 。
   Give me a call when you are free.
   你有空给我打电话吧。

2. Ngo5 ci4 • di1 ko1 nei5 laa1.
   我 遲 啲 call 你 啦 。
   I will call you later.
   我待会儿给你打电话吧。

6.3.3 Verb '*look for*' : wan2 搵 *(Track 123)*

When meaning *to find*, "wan2 搵" is similar to "找" in Putonghua. However, "wan2 搵" does not express "to give change" as in "找錢" in Putonghua.

P zhǎo 找

Examples:

1. Jau5 jan4 wan2 nei5 aa3 !
   有 人 搵 你 呀 ！
   Someone is looking for you.
   有人找你！

2. Ngo5 soeng2 hai2 Hoeng1 • gong2 wan2 • gung1.
   我 想 喺 香 港 搵 工 。
   I want to find a job in Hong Kong.
   我想在香港找工作。

6.3.4 '(*Someone*) *is in*' : hai2 • dou6 喺度 *(Track 124)*

The Cantonese verb "hai2 喺" is used to denote the location of a person or thing, equivalent to "在" in Putonghua. When it is used to mean "*someone is in*", Putonghua "在" can be used on its own like "她在". However "hai2 喺" must accompany a place word such as "uk1 • kei2 屋企". In case the place is understood from the context, the generic locative term "dou6 度" follows "hai2 喺", meaning someone or something is "here / there / in".

Examples:

1. *Q:* Can4 siu2 • ze2 hai2 m4 hai2 • dou6 aa3 ?
   陳 小 姐 喺 唔 喺 度 呀 ？
   Is Miss Chan in?
   陈小姐在吗？

   A: Keoi5 hai2 • dou6, m4 • goi1 dang2 dang2.
   佢 喺 度 ， 唔 該 等 等 。
   Yes *she is, please wait.*
   她在，麻烦你等一下。

2. *Q:* Keoi5 hai2 m4 hai2 uk1 • kei2 aa3 ?
   佢 喺 唔 喺 屋 企 呀 ？
   Is she at home?
   她在家吗？

   A: Keoi5 m4 hai2 uk1 • kei2.
   佢 唔 喺 屋 企 。
   She is not at home.
   她不在家。

6.3.5 '*When*' questions : gei2 • si4 幾時 *(Track 125)*

To ask the when questions, "gei2 • si4 幾時" is put between the subject and verb phrase.

P shénme shíhou 什么 时候

The following are the suggested answers to the '*when*' questions.

a) Days:

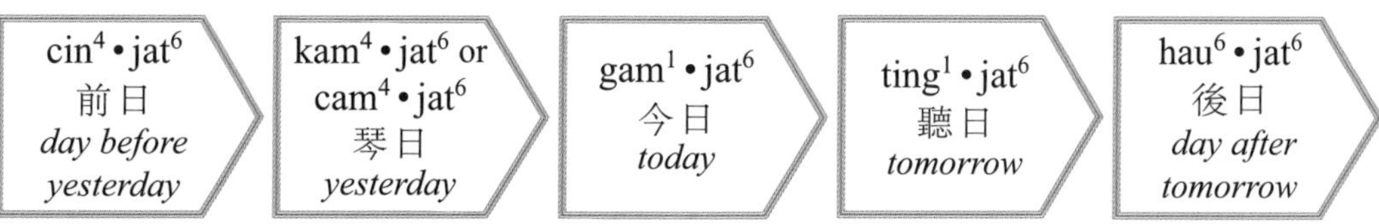

b) Weeks:

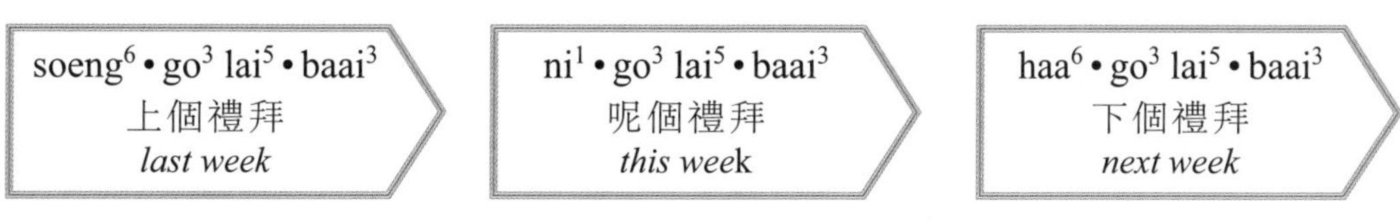

c) Months:

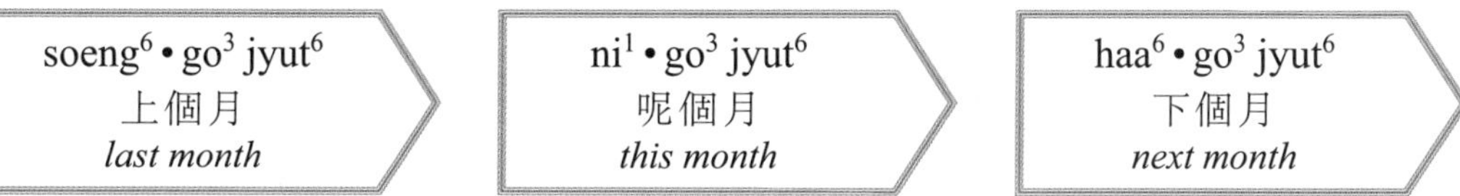

d) Years:

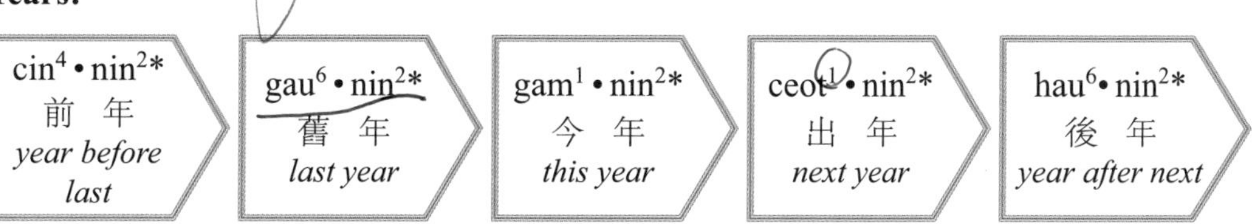

Examples:

1. Nei⁵ gei² • si⁴ saang¹ • jat⁶ aa³?
   你 幾 時 生 日 呀 ？
   When is your birthday?
   你 什 么 时 候 生 日 ？

2. Ngo⁵ haa⁶ • go³ lai⁵ • baai³ • jat¹ saang¹ • jat⁶.
   我 下 個 禮 拜 一 生 日 。
   My birthday is next Monday.
   我 下 个 礼 拜 一 生 日 。

6.3.6 '*Meet someone at some place*': hai² 喺 + *place* + dang² 等 + *person*

[Track 126]

To meet someone somewhere, the sentence order is "hai² 喺 (*at*) + place + dang² 等 (*wait*)" + person.

Sometimes gin³ 見 (*see*) is used instead of dang² 等.

P zài…děng / jiàn
在 … 等 / 見

Examples:

1. Hai^{2} bin^{1} • dou^{6} dang^{2} nei^{5} aa^{3}?
   喺 邊 度 等 你 呀 ？
   Where shall I meet you?
   在哪儿等你呢？

2. Hai^{2} hok^{6} • haau^{6} mun^{4} • hau^{2} gin^{3} laa^{1}.
   喺 學 校 門 口 見 啦 。
   Let's meet in front of the school main gate.
   在学校大门口见吧。

6.3.7 Verb suffix '*back*' : faan^{1} 返 (Track 127)

To express the meaning of '*back*', "faan^{1} 返" is added after a verb.

Examples:

1. Ngo^{5} ji^{4} • gaa^{1} m^{4} dak^{1} • haan^{4}, jat^{1} • zan^{6} daa^{2} • faan^{1} din^{6} • waa^{2*} bei^{2} nei^{5} laa^{1}.
   我 而 家 唔 得 閒 ， 一 陣 打 返 電 話 俾 你 啦 。
   I am not free right now. I'll call you back later.
   我现在没空，待会儿给你回电话。

2. Ngo^{5} bei^{2} • faan^{1} cin^{2*} nei^{5} aa^{1}.
   我 俾 返 錢 你 吖 。
   I'll give the money back to you.
   我把钱还给你。

6.4 Cantonese tones :

There are six tones in Cantonese. Each tone indicates a pitch or pitch contour of a syllable. Syllables with the same initial and final, but with different tones will have different meanings.

(a) upper tones : (Track 128)

1. Hoeng^{1} 香	gong^{2} 港	leng^{3} 靚	*Hong Kong is beautiful*
2. saam^{1} 三	dim^{2} 點	bun^{3} 半	*half past three*
3. siu^{1} 燒	ngo^{2*} 鵝	gwai^{3} 貴	*roast goose is expensive*

(b) lower tones: *(Track 129)*

1.	ngau^4 牛	naam^5 腩	min^6 麪	*brisket noodle*
2.	naan^4 難	maai^5 買	maai^6 賣	*difficult to buy and sell*
3.	m^4 唔	tou^5 肚	ngo^6 餓	*not hungry*

(c) six tones: *(Track 130)*

1	2	3	4	5	6
si^1 詩 *poetry*	si^2 史 *history*	si^3 試 *try*	si^4 時 *time*	si^5 市 *market*	si^6 是 *be*
fu^1 夫 *husband*	fu^2 苦 *bitter*	fu^3 褲 *trousers*	fu^4 符 *symbol*	fu^5 婦 *woman*	fu^6 負 *negative*
yat^1 一 *one*	gau^2 九 *nine*	baat^3 八 *eight*	ling^4 零 *zero*	ng^5 五 *five*	ji^6 二 *two*

6.5 Supplementary Vocabulary

6.5.1 Looking for someone on the phone: *(Track 131)*

(a) M^4 • goi^1 nei^5 giu^3 + (*person*) + teng^1 din^6 • waa^{2*}.

唔 該 你 叫 . . . 聽 電 話 。

May I speak with ... please.

麻 烦 你 请 . . . 接 电 话 。

(b) Ceng^2 • man^6 + (*person*) + hai^2 m^4 hai^2 • dou^6 aa^3?

請 問 . . . 喺 唔 喺 度 呀 ？

Excuse me, is ... in?

请 问 . . . 在 吗 ？

(c) M^{4} • goi^{1} + (*person*) + aa^{1}.

唔 該 ... 吖 ！

Can I speak with ..., please?

请叫 ... 接电话！

(d) (*person*) + aa^{1}, m^{4} • goi^{1}.

... 吖 ， 唔 該 ！

Can I speak with ..., please?

请叫 ... 接电话！

6.5.2 Answering the phone: *(Track 132)*

(a) Nei^{5} sik^{1} m^{4} sik^{1} gong^{2} Jing^{1} • man^{2*} aa^{3}?

你 識 唔 識 講 英 文 呀 ？

Can you speak English?

你会说英文吗？

(b) Ngo^{5} hai^{6}.

我 係 。

This is he/she (speaking).

我就是。

(c) M^{4} • goi^{1} dang^{2} dang^{2}.

唔 該 等 等 。

Please hold on.

麻烦你等一下。

(d) Keoi^{5} m^{4} hai^{2} • dou^{6}.

佢 唔 喺 度 。

He/she's not in.

他/她不在。

(e) M^{4} • hou^{2} • ji^{3} • si^{3}, mou^{5} hing^{3} • ceoi^{3}.

唔 好 意 思 ， 冇 興 趣 。

Sorry, I am not interested. (as a reply to telephone sales)

不好意思，没有兴趣。

(f) Ceng2 • man6 bin1 • wai2* aa3?
請 問 邊 位 呀 ？
Who's calling, please?
请 问 你 是 哪 位 ？

6.5.3 Dates: *(Track 133)*

In Cantonese, year, month, and day always appear in this order.

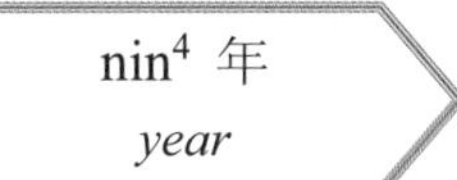

jyut6 月 *month*

hou6 號 *day*

1. **Ji6 ling4 jat1 jat1** **nin4** **sap6 • ji6 • jyut6** **ji6 • sap6 • ng5** **hou6**
二 零 一 一 年 十 二 月 二 十 五 號
2 0 0 1 year twelfth month twenty-fifth day
December 25, 2010.

2. **Jat1 gau2 gau2 cat1** **nin4** **cat1 • jyut6** **jat1** **hou6**
一 九 九 七 年 七 月 一 號
1 9 9 7 year seventh month first day
*July 1, 1997**

†† * The day of Hong Kong's handover to China.

6.5.4 MTR stations in Hong Kong *(Track 134)*

No.	Cantonese Romanization	Chinese	Putonghua Romanization	English
1.	Zung1 • waan4	中環	Zhōnghuán 中环	Central
2.	Hung4 • ham3	紅磡	Hóngkàn 红磡	Hung Hom
3.	Gau2 • lung4 • tong4	九龍塘	Jiǔlóngtáng 九龙塘	Kowloon Tong
4.	Lo4 • wu4	羅湖	Luóhú 罗湖	Lo Wu
5.	Wong6 • gok3	旺角	Wàngjiǎo 旺角	Mong Kok
6.	Taai3 • zi2	太子	Tàizǐ 太子	Prince Edward
7.	Zak1 • jyu4 • cung1	鰂魚涌	Zéyúchōng 鲗鱼涌	Quarry Bay
8.	Zim1 • saa1 • zeoi2	尖沙咀	Jiānshāzuǐ 尖沙咀	Tsim Sha Tsui
9.	Cyun4 • waan1	荃灣	Quánwān 荃湾	Tsuen Wan
10.	Daai6 • hok6	大學	Dàxué 大学	University

6.6 Exercise

6.6.1 Matching

1.	m^4 dak^1 唔得	______	A. free
2.	ni^1 paai^{2*} 呢排	______	B. not okay
3.	do^1 di^1 多啲	______	C. still want to
4.	zung^6 soeng^2 仲想	______	D. recently
5.	dak^1•haan^4 得閒	______	E. more

6.6.2 Multiple choice

1. *Do you have anything important to speak with him about?*

   Nei^5 你 jau^5 有 mou^5 冇 ____________ si^6 事 wan^2 搵 keoi^5 佢 aa^3 呀？

   A. jiu^3 gan^2 要緊 B. gan^2•jiu^3 緊要 C. soeng^2 jiu^3 想要

2. *Call me tomorrow.*

   Ting^1•jat^6 聽日 ____________ 。

   A. bei^2 ngo^5 daa^2 din^6•waa^{2*} 俾我打電話

   B. daa^2 bei^2 ngo^5 din^6•waa^{2*} 打俾我電話

   C. daa^2 din^6•waa^{2*} bei^2 ngo^5 打電話俾我

3. *Is Mr. Chan in?*

   Can^4 陳 saang^1 生 ______ aa^3 呀？

   A. hai^2 m^4 hai^2•dou^6 喺唔喺度 B. hai^2 m^4 hai^2 喺唔喺

   C. dou^6 hai^2 m^4 hai^2 度喺唔喺

4. *He wants to earn more money.*

   Keoi^5 佢 soeng^2 想 wan^2 搵 ____________ cin^{2*} 錢。

   A. do^1 dei^6 多哋 B. do^1 dim^2 多點 C. do^1 di^1 多啲

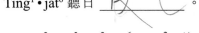

5. *When will you go?*

Nei^{5} 你 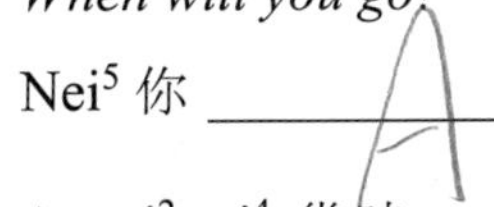 heoi^{3} 去 aa^{3} 呀？

A. gei^{2} • si^{4} 幾時　　B. gei^{2} jat^{6} 幾日　　C. gei^{2} • do^{1} jat^{6} 幾多日

6.6.3 Sentence order

Rearrange the words in the correct order as in shown the example.

Example :

I'll go to Sha Tin with my classmate.

heoi^{3} 去	tung^{4} 同	ngo^{5} 我	Saa^{1} • tin^{4} 沙田	tung^{4} • hok^{6} 同學
(4)	(2)	(1)	(5)	(3)

1. *I'll see you in front of the MTR station.*

nei^{5} 你	dang^{2} 等	hai^{2} 喺	cin^{4} • min^{6} 前面	dei^{6} • tit^{3} zaam^{6} 地鐵站
(1)	(5)	(2)	(4)	(3)

2. *I came on the 1st of August this year.*

ngo^{5} 我	lei^{4} 嚟	jat^{1} hou^{6} 一號	baat^{3} • jyut^{6} 八月	gam^{1} • nin^{2*} 今年
(1)	(5)	(4)	(3)	(2)

3. *Do you speak English?*

sik^{1} 識	gong^{2} 講	aa^{3} 呀	m^{4} sik^{1} 唔識	Jing^{1} • man^{2*} 英文
(1)	(3)	(5)	(2)	(4)

4. *I'll call you back later.*

faan^{1} 返	daa^{2} 打	bei^{2} nei^{5} 俾你	din^{6} • waa^{2*} 電話	ci^{4} • di^{1} 遲啲
( ) 3	( ) 2	( ) 5	( ) 4	( ) 1

5. *We go and eat dimsum today.*

sik^{6} 食	heoi^{3} 去	ngo^{5} • dei^{6} 我哋	gam^{1} • jat^{6} 今日	dim^{2} • sam^{1} 點心
(4)	(3)	(1)	(2)	(5)

7

Sik^6 dim^2 • sam^1

食點心 *Having dim sum*

Learning Tasks

- to talk with the receptionist
- to order Chinese tea
- to order Cantonese dim sum
- to order Cantonese desserts
- to ask for the bill
- to talk about personal experience

Language Focus

- '*yes-no*' questions for two syllable words: A + m^4 唔 + AB + aa^3 呀 ?
- '*no preference*': mou^5 • so^2 • wai^6 冇所謂
- classifiers (2)
- '*universal affirmation*': wh-word + dou^1 都 + affirmation
- comparison of two items: gwo^3 過
- degree adverbs: do^1 多 / siu^2 少
- resultative state '*full*' : baau^2 飽
- particle to indicate '*completion of process*' : maai^4 埋

Sounds and Tones

- Putonghua & Cantonese initials in comparison

Supplementary Vocabulary

- Cantonese dim sum
- Chinese tea
- Chinese desserts
- kitchen utensils

Exercise

- matching
- multiple choice
- comprehension

 7.1 Vocabulary *(Track 135)*

No.	Cantonese Romanization	Cantonese Characters	Putonghua & Chinese Characters	English
1.	a) gei^{2} wai^{2*}	幾位	jǐ wèi 几位	how many people (wai^{2*} : formal classifier for persons)
	b) ng^{5} wai^{2*}	五位	wǔ wèi 五位	five people
2.	a) sing^{3}	姓	xìng 姓	surname
	b) sing^{3} Can^{4}	姓陳	xìng Chén 姓陈	surnamed Chan
3.	a) hou^{6} • maa^{5}	號碼	hàomǎ 号码	number
	b) saam^{3} • sap^{6} • jat^{1} hou^{6}	三十一號	sānshíyī hào 三十一号	number thirty one
4.	a) giu^{3}	叫	jiào 叫	call
	b) dang^{2} giu^{3} hou^{6} • maa^{5}	等叫號碼	děng jiào hàomǎ 等叫号码	wait for your number to be called
5.	a) zung^{1} • ji^{3}	鍾意	xǐhuan 喜欢	like
	b) m^{4} zung^{1} • ji^{3}	唔鍾意	bù xǐhuan 不喜欢	do not like
	c) zung^{1} m^{4} zung^{1} • ji^{3}	鍾唔鍾意	xǐhuan bù xǐhuan 喜欢不喜欢	do you like it or not
	d) zung^{1} • ji^{3} jam^{2} me^{1} caa^{4}	鍾意飲咩茶	xǐhuan hē shénme chá 喜欢喝什么茶	what kind of tea would you like to have?
6.	mou^{5} • so^{2} • wai^{6}	無所謂	wúsuǒwèi 无所谓	anything would do
7.	jat^{1} wu^{4}	一壺	yì hú 一壶	a pot (of tea, water) (wu^{4} : classifier for liquids in a teapot)
8.	pou^{2} • nei^{2}	普洱	pǔ'ěr 普洱	Puer (tea)
9.	gwan^{2} • seoi^{2}	滾水	rè kāishuǐ 热开水	hot water
10.	a) dim^{2} • sam^{1}	點心	diǎnxīn 点心	dim sum
	b) sik^{6} me^{1} dim^{2} • sam^{1}	食咩點心	chī shénme diǎnxīn 吃什么点心	what dim sum do you eat?

11.	a) me^{1}… dou^{1}…	咩…都…	shénme…dōu… 什么…都…	no matter what (used to express inclusiveness)
	b) me^{1} dim^{2} • sam^{1} dou^{1} zung^{1} • ji^{3} sik^{6}	咩點心都鍾意食	shénme diǎnxīn dōu xǐhuan chī 什么点心都喜欢吃	I like all kinds of dim sum
12.	haa^{1} • gaau^{2}	蝦餃	xiā jiǎo 虾饺	shrimp dumplings
13.	siu^{1} • maai^{2*}	燒賣	shāomai 烧卖	pork dumplings
14.	caa^{1} • siu^{1} • baau^{1}	叉燒包	chāshāo bāo 叉烧包	BBQ pork buns
15.	ceon^{1} • gyun^{2}	春卷	chūn juǎn 春卷	spring rolls
16.	a) loeng^{5} lung^{4}	兩籠	liǎng lóng 两笼	two steamers (of dim sum) (lung^{4} : classifier for dim sum)
	b) giu^{3} do^{1} loeng^{5} lung^{4}	叫多兩籠	duō jiào liǎng lóng 多叫两笼	order two more steamers (of dim sum)
17.	a) (adj) • gwo^{3} +…	(形) • 過…	bǐ…(adj) 比…(形)	more (adj) than…
	b) hou^{2} • sik^{6} • gwo^{3} hok^{6} • haau^{6} ge^{3} dim^{2} • sam^{1}	好食過學校嘅點心	bǐ xuéxiào de diǎnxīn hǎochī 比学校的点心好吃	more tasty than the dim sum served in school
	c) ni^{1} • di^{1} dim^{2} • sam^{1} hou^{2} • sik^{6} • gwo^{3} hok^{6} • haau^{6} ge^{3} dim^{2} • sam^{1}	呢啲點心好食過學校嘅點心	zhèxiē diǎnxīn bǐ xuéxiào de diǎnxīn hǎochī 这些点心比学校的点心好吃	these dim sum are more tasty than those served in school
18.	a) do^{1}	多	duō 多	many / much
	b) hou^{2} do^{1}	好多	hěn duō 很多	so many / much
	c) sik^{6} do^{1} di^{1}	食多啲	duō chī yìdiǎn 多吃一点	eat more
19.	a) sik^{6} • baau^{2}	食飽	chībǎo 吃饱	eat enough
	b) mei^{6} sik^{6} • baau^{2}	未食飽	hái méiyǒu chī bǎo 还没有吃饱	have not eaten enough yet
	c) sik^{6} • baau^{2} mei^{6} aa^{3}	食飽未呀	chī bǎole méiyǒu 吃饱了没有	are you full yet?

20.	zung^{6} • jau^{5}	仲有…	hái yǒu 还有…	there is /are still…
21.	a) maai^{4}	埋	diào 掉	(used after a verb) express completion
	b) sik^{6} • maai^{4} keoi^{5}	食埋佢	bǎ tā chīdiào 把它吃掉	finish eating it, eat it up
22.	tim^{4} • ban^{2}	甜品	tiánpǐn 甜品	desserts
23.	mong^{1} • gwo^{2} bou^{3} • din^{1}	芒果布甸	mángguǒ bùdīng 芒果布丁	mango pudding
24.	sai^{1} • mai^{5} • lou^{6}	西米露	xīmǐlù 西米露	coconut milk with sago
25.	maai^{4} • daan^{1}	埋單	jiézhàng 结账	pay the bill

7.2 Ka-Man, Tai-Lung, Ka-Nam and Wing-sze arrive at the dim sum house. *(Track 136)*

Gei^{2} wai^{2*} aa^{3}?
幾 位 呀 ？
How many people?
几 位 ？

Sei^{3} wai^{2}.
四 位 。
Four people.
四 位 。

Gwai^{3} sing^{3} aa^{3}?
貴 姓 呀 ？
May I have your surname, please?
贵 姓 呀 ？

Sing^{3} Can^{4}.
姓 陳 。
My surname is Chan.
姓 陈 。

Can^{4} siu^{2} • ze^{2}, dang^{2} giu^{3} hou^{6} • maa^{5} laa^{1}!
陳 小 姐 ， 等 叫 號 碼 啦 ！
Miss Chan, please wait for your number !
陈 小 姐 ， 等 叫 你 的 号 码 吧 ！

M^{4} • goi^{1}.
唔 該 。
Thank you.
谢谢。

Twenty minutes later

Saam^{3} • sap^{6} • jat^{1} hou^{6}, Can^{4} siu^{2} • ze^{2}.
三 十 一 號 ， 陳 小 姐 。
Number thirty one, Miss Chan.
三十一号，陈小姐。

M^{4} • goi^{1}.
唔 該 。
Thank you.
谢谢。

They sit down at the table

Nei^{5} • dei^{6} zung^{1} • ji^{3} jam^{2} me^{1} caa^{4} aa^{3}?
你 哋 鍾 意 飲 咩 茶 呀 ？
What kind of tea would you like to drink?
你们喜欢喝什么茶？

Mou^{5} • so^{2} • wai^{6}.
無 所 謂 。
Anything would do.
无所谓。

Gam^{2}, jat^{1} wu^{4} pou^{2} • nei^{2}, jat^{1} wu^{4} gwan^{2} • seoi^{2} laa^{1}!
噉 ， 一 壺 普 洱 ， 一 壺 滾 水 啦 ！
Let's have a pot of Puer and a pot of hot water then!
那么，一壶普洱，一壶热开水吧！！

Nei^{5} • dei^{6} soeng^{2} sik^{6} me^{1} dim^{2} • sam^{1} aa^{3}?
你 哋 想 食 咩 點 心 呀 ？
What dim sum would you like to eat?
你们想吃什么点心？

Ngo5 me1 dim2 • sam1 dou1 zung1 • ji3 sik6.
我 咩 點 心 都 鍾 意 食 。
I like all kinds of Dim Sum.
我什么点心都喜欢吃。

Nei5 • dei6 zung1 m4 zung1 • ji3 sik6 haa1 • gaau2, siu1 • maai2*, caa1 • siu1 • baau1, ceon1 • gyun2 aa3?
你 哋 鍾 唔 鍾 意 食 蝦 餃 、 燒 賣 、 叉 燒 包 、 春 卷 呀 ？
Do you like shrimp dumplings, pork dumplings, BBQ pork buns and spring rolls?
你们喜欢不喜欢吃虾饺、烧卖、叉烧包、春卷？

Zung1 • ji3.
鍾 意 。
Yes, I do.
喜欢。

Ngo5 hou2 zung1 • ji3 sik6 caa1 • siu1 • baau1, soeng2 jiu1 do1 loeng5 lung4.
我 好 鍾 意 食 叉 燒 包 ， 想 要 多 兩 籠 。
I like BBQ pork dumplings very much. I want to order two more steamers of them.
我很喜欢吃叉烧包，想多要两笼。

Gam2, giu3 do1 loeng5 lung4 laa1.
噉 ， 叫 多 兩 籠 啦 。
Let's order two more then.
那，多叫两笼吧。

After eating, there are still some dim sum on the table

Dim2 • sam1 hou2 m4 hou2 • sik6 aa3?
點 心 好 唔 好 食 呀 ？
How are the Dim Sum?
点心好吃不好吃？

Ni1 di1 dim2 • sam1 hou2 • sik6 • gwo3 hok6 • haau6 ge3 dim2 • sam1 hou2 do1.
呢 啲 點 心 好 食 過 學 校 嘅 點 心 好 多 。
These Dim Sum are much better than those served in school.
这些点心比学校的点心好吃多了。

Gam2, sik6 do1 di1 laa1.
噉 ， 食 多 啲 啦 。
Then eat some more.
那，多吃一点吧。

Nei5 • dei6 sik6 • baau2 mei6 aa3?
你 哋 食 飽 未 呀 ？
Is that enough food for you?
你們吃饱了吗？

Sik6 • baau2 laa3.
食 飽 喇 。
I'm full now.
吃饱了。

Zung6 • jau5 di1 caa1 • siu1 • baau1, faai3 di1 sik6 • maai4 keoi5 laa1.
仲 有 啲 叉 燒 包 ， 快 點 食 埋 佢 啦 。
We have some BBQ pork bun left. Quick, eat it up.
还有些叉烧包，快点食掉它吧。

Sik6 m4 sik6 tim4 • ban2 aa3?
食 唔 食 甜 品 呀 ？
Anyone eating desserts?
吃甜品吗？

Ngo5 jiu3 mong1 • gwo2 bou3 • din1.
我 要 芒 果 布 甸 。
I want a mango pudding.
我要吃芒果布丁。

Ngo5 jiu3 sai1 • mai5 • lou6.
我 要 西 米 露 。
I'll have some coconut milk with sago.
我要西米露。

After finishing the desserts, Ka-Man asks for the bill.

M4 • goi1 maai4 • daan1!
唔 該 埋 單 ！
May I have the bill, please?
请结账！

7.3 Grammar Notes

7.3.1 '*Yes-no*' question for two-syllable words: A + m⁴ 唔 + AB + aa³ 呀 ? *(Track 137)*

The 'yes-no' type question is expressed with the positive and the negative forms combined together, as in 'A + m⁴ A'. With verbs or adjectives made up of two syllables, the same rule applies, but the second syllable only appears in the negative form, as in 'A + m⁴ AB'. Note that Putonghua typically takes the pattern 'AB + bù + AB'.

P AB + bù 不 + AB?

Examples:

1. *A:* Nei⁵ hoi¹ m⁴ hoi¹ • sam¹ aa³?
   你 開 唔 開 心 呀 ？
   Are you happy?
   你高兴不高兴？

   B: Hou² hoi¹ • sam¹.
   好 開 心 。
   Very happy.
   很高兴。

2. *A:* Keoi⁵ • dei⁶ tiu³ m⁴ tiu³ mou⁵ aa³?
   佢 哋 跳 唔 跳 舞 呀 ？
   Will they dance?
   他们跳舞不跳舞？

   B: M⁴ tiu³ mou⁵.
   唔 跳 舞 。
   No.
   不跳舞。

7.3.2 '*No preference*' : mou⁵ • so² • wai⁶ 冇所謂 *(Track 138)*

When you are asked to choose, but have no preference, the following idiomatic expression can be used: "mou⁵ • so² • wai⁶ 冇所謂". You can also repeat the question followed by "dou¹ mou⁵ • so² • wai⁶ 都冇所謂" or "dou¹ dak¹ 都得".

P wúsuǒwèi 无所谓
dōu xíng 都行

Examples:

1. Sik⁶ me¹ dou¹ mou⁵ • so² • wai⁶.
   食 咩 都 冇 所 謂 。
   Any food would be fine by me.
   吃什么都无所谓。

2. Heoi³ bin¹ • dou⁶ dou¹ dak¹.
   去 邊 度 都 得 。
   Whenever you want to go is okay.
   去哪儿都行。

7.3.3 Classifiers (2) : *(Track 139)*

In unit 3.3.3, we learned ten common classifiers. In this unit, we will learn ten more frequently-used classifiers. Note that except for the first three (wai2, bou6 and gau6), these classifiers are all terms of containers that are used as classifiers.

wai2*	位	for persons. (used in formal situations)
bou6	部	for small machines or books such as mobile phones, computers, television sets, books, dictionaries, etc.
gau6	嚿	for pieces or lumps of meat, money, clouds, rocks, etc.
bui1	杯	for drinks poured in cups or glasses.
zeon1	樽	for drinks poured in bottles, oil stored in bottles, etc.
wun2	碗	for rice, soup, noodles, porridge served in bowls.
dip6	碟	for cooked food served on plates.
lung4	籠	for cooked food served in bamboo steamers, or birds kept in a cage.
wu4	壺	for tea and water served in pots.
gun3	罐	for beer, soft drink, milk powder, ham, etc. in cans.

Examples:

C		P		E
jat1 wai2*	一位	yí wèi	一位	a person
jat1 bui1 seoi2	一杯水	yì bēi shuǐ	一杯水	a glass of water
jat1 wun2 faan6	一碗飯	yì wǎn fàn	一碗饭	a bowl of rice
jat1 dip6 coi3	一碟菜	yì pán cài	一盘菜	a dish of vegetables
jat1 lung4 haa1 • gaau2	一籠蝦餃	yì lóng xiā jiǎo	一笼虾饺	a steamer of shrimp dumplings
jat1 wu4 caa4	一壺茶	yì hú chá	一壶茶	a pot of tea
jat1 zeon1 hei3 • seoi2	一樽汽水	yì píng qìshuǐ	一瓶汽水	a bottle of soft drink
jat1 gun3 be1 • zau2	一罐啤酒	yí guàn píjiǔ	一罐啤酒	a can of beer
jat1 bou6 sau2 • gei1	一部手機	yí bù shǒujī	一部手机	a mobile phone
jat1 gau6 siu1 • maai2*	一嚿燒賣	yì kē shāomai	一颗烧卖	a piece of pork dumpling

7.3.4 *'Universal affirmation'* : wh-word + dou1 都 + affirmation (Track 140)

The combination of "wh-question word + dou1 都 (*all*)" expresses universal affirmation. Thus "mat1 • je5 乜嘢 (*what*) / bin1 • go3 邊個 (*who*) / bin1 • dou6 邊度 (*where*) / gei2 • si4 幾時 (*when*)" + dou1 都 (*all*) imply anything, anyone, anywhere, anytime respectively.

P shénme…dōu 什么…都
shuí…dōu 谁…都
nǎlǐ…dōu 哪里…都
shéme shíhou…dōu
什么时候…都

Examples:

1. Ngo5 mat1 • je5 dou1 soeng2 maai5.
   我 乜 嘢 都 想 買 。
   I want to buy everything.
   我什么都想买。

2. Bin1 • go3 dou1 zi1 laa1.
   邊 個 都 知 啦 。
   Everyone knows.
   谁都知道。

7.3.5 Comparison of two objects : gwo3 過 (Track 141)

When comparing two items, the pattern "(adj) + gwo3 過 (*than*) + object of comparison" is used. The degree can be expressed after the object of comparison by adding "hou2 do1 好多 (*a lot*)" or "siu2 • siu2 少少 (*little*)".

P bǐ 比 + object of comparison + adjective

A + adj + 过 gwo3 + B

Examples:

1. Nei5 hou2 • gwo3 keoi5 hou2 do1.
   你 好 過 佢 好 多 。
   You are a lot better than him.
   你比他好很多。

2. Ni1 go3 gwai3 • gwo3 go2 go3 siu2 • siu2.
   呢 個 貴 過 嗰 個 少 少 。
   This one is a little more expensive than that one.
   这个比那个贵一点。

7.3.6 Degree adverbs : do1 多 / siu2 少 *(Track 142)*

In Cantonese the adverb "do1 多 (*many*)" or "siu2 少 (*little*)" is put right after a verb to express doing something more or less. Note that the order is reversed in Putonghua.

P duō 多 / shǎo 少 + verb

Examples:

1. Gong2 do1 di1 Gwong2 • dung1 • waa2* laa1.
   講 多 啲 廣 東 話 啦 。
   Speak more Cantonese .
   多说广东话。

2. Nei5 waa6 gaam2 • fei4, sik6 siu2 di1 laa1.
   你 話 減 肥 ， 食 少 啲 啦 。
   You said you are on diet, you should eat less.
   你说要减肥，少吃点吧。

7.3.7 Resultative state '*full*' : baau2 飽 *(Track 143)*

To express the state "full" or "enough" as a result of eating, "baau2 飽" is added after "sik6 食 (*eat*)". The meaning of "baau2 飽" can be metaphorically extended to other verbs, such as "faan3 瞓 (*sleep*)" or "siu3 笑 (*laugh*)", implying that the action has reached a satisfactory level.

P verb + bǎo 飽

Examples:

1. Siu3 dou1 siu3 • baau2 laa1, m4 • sai2 sik6 laa1.
   笑 都 笑 飽 啦 ， 唔 駛 食 啦 。
   You laughed so much that you don't need to eat any more.
   笑都笑饱啦，不用吃了。

2. Sik6 • baau2 zau6 fan3, fan3 • baau2 zau6 sik6.
   食 飽 就 瞓 ， 瞓 飽 就 食 。
   All you do is eat and sleep, then eat and sleep more.
   吃饱就睡，睡饱就吃。

7.3.8 Particle to indicate '*completion of process*' : maai4 埋 *(Track 144)*

"Maai4 埋" is attached to a verb to indicate the completion of the whole process by finishing the remaining task.

Examples:

1. Nei^{5} giu^{3} • zo^{2} gam^{3} do^{1} je^{5} sik^{6}, faai^{3} di^{1} sik^{6} • maai^{4} keoi^{5} laa^{1}.
   你 叫 咗 咁 多 嘢 食 ， 快 啲 食 埋 佢 啦 。
   You ordered so much food, so hurry up and eat them up.
   你点了这么多东西吃，赶快吃掉。

2. Nei^{5} zau^{2} sin^{1} laa^{1}, ngo^{5} jiu^{3} zou^{6} • maai^{4} di^{1} je^{5}.
   你 走 先 啦 ， 我 要 做 埋 啲 嘢 。
   Why don't you go home now, I still have something that needs finishing.
   你先走吧，我要把工作做完。

7.4 Cantonese and Putonghua initials in comparison :

Both Cantonese and Putonghua come from the same ancestor, which results in their sharing a great number of phonetic features. One such feature is the same initial sound found in Cantonese and Putonghua, as in the following pairs. *(Track 145)*

Putonghua	Chinese characters	Cantonese
bà	爸	baa^{1}
pà	怕	paa^{3}
mā	媽	maa^{1}
fàn	飯	faan^{6}
dà	大	daai^{6}

Putonghua	Chinese characters	Cantonese
tài	太	taai^{3}
nǎi	奶	naai^{5}
la^{1}	拉	laai^{1}
gāo	高	gou^{1}
kàng	抗	kong^{3}

Putonghua	Chinese characters	Cantonese
hǎi	海	hoi^{2}
zǎo	早	zou^{2}
cān	餐	caan^{1}
sòng	送	sung^{3}
wàng	旺	wong^{6}

Sometimes same or similar sounds may be spelt differently, but you can convert from Putonghua to Cantonese if you know the following rules.

1	Putonghua "z, c, s", "zh, ch, sh" and partial "j, q, x" correspond to Cantonese "z, c, s".
2	Putonghua "gu" and "ku" are often spelt as "gw" and "kw" in Cantonese.
3	Putonghua "y" is similiar to Cantonese "j" .

There are times when you come across irregular cases. The table below displays some of the frequently found irregular cases for your reference. *(Track 146)*

Putonghua	Chinese characters	Cantonese
bèi	倍	pui^{5}
pí	啤	be^{1}
tè	特	dak^{6}
kē	科	fo^{1}
kāi	開	hoi^{1}

Putonghua	Chinese characters	Cantonese
huá	華	waa^{4}
huǒ	火	fo^{2}
jiàn	見	gin^{3}
qiáng	強	koeng^{4}
qǐ	起	hei^{2}

Putonghua	Chinese characters	Cantonese
xiā	蝦	haa^{1}
rén	人	jan^{4}
wǎn	晚	maan^{5}
yá	牙	ngaa^{4}

7.5 Supplementary Vocabulary

7.5.1 Cantonese dim sum: *(Track 147)*

haa^{1} • gaau^{2}
蝦 餃
steamed shrimp dumpling

siu^{1} • maai^{2*}
燒 賣
steamed pork dumpling

caa^{1} • siu^{1} • baau^{1}
叉 燒 飽
BBQ pork bun

ceon^{1} • gyun^{2}
春 卷
spring roll

ceong^{2*} • fan^{2}
腸 粉
steamed rice roll

paai^{4} • gwat^{1}
排 骨
spare ribs

haam^{4} • seoi^{2} • gok^{2*}
鹹 水 角
deep fried mixed dumpling

sin^{1} • zuk^{1} • gyun^{2}
鮮 竹 卷
bean curd roll

fan^{2} • gwo^{2}
粉 果
steamed pork dumpling

fung^{6} • zaau^{2}
鳳 爪
chicken feet

caa^{1} • siu^{1} • sou^{1}
叉 燒 酥
BBQ pork puffs

lo^{4} • baak^{6} • gou^{1}
蘿 蔔 糕
oriental radish cake

7.5.2 Chinese tea *(Track 148)*

No.	Cantonese Romanization	Chinese	Putonghua Romanization	English
1.	guk^{1} • faa^{1}	菊花	júhuā 菊花	Chrysanthemum
2.	hoeng^{1} • pin^{2*}	香片	mòlihuāchá 茉莉花茶	Jasmine
3.	sau^{6} • mei^{2*}	壽眉	shòuméi 寿眉	Shou Mei
4.	seoi^{2} • sin^{1}	水仙	shuǐxiān 水仙	Shui-Hsien
5.	tit^{3} • gun^{1} • jam^{1}	鐵觀音	tiěguānyīn 铁观音	T'ieh-Kuan-Yin

7.5.3 Chinese deserts *(Track 149)*

No.	Cantonese Romanization	Chinese	Putonghua Romanization	English
1.	maa^5 • dau^6 • gou^1	馬豆糕	mădòugāo 马豆糕	coconut & yellow pea cake
2.	lau^4 • lin^4 baan^1 • kik^1	榴槤班戟	liúlián bānjǐ 榴莲班戟	durian pancake
3.	naai^5 • wong^4 • baau^1	奶黃包	nǎihuángbāo 奶黄包	milk & egg custard buns
4.	daan^6 • taat^1	蛋撻	dàntǎ 蛋挞	egg tart
5.	saang^1 • gwo^2 pun^2	生果盤	shuǐguǒpán 水果盘	fruit platter
6.	joeng^4 • zi^1 • gam^1 • lou^6	楊枝甘露	yángzhī gānlù 杨枝甘露	mango desert with pomelo & sago
7.	hung^4 • dau^{2*} • saa^1	紅豆沙	hóngdòushā 红豆沙	red bean soup
8.	zin^1 • deoi^1	煎堆	jiānduī 煎堆	sesame balls
9.	dau^6 • fu^6 • faa^1	豆腐花	dòufuhuā 豆腐花	tofu pudding
10.	hap^6 • tou^4 wu^{2*}	合桃糊	hétáohú 核桃糊	walnut paste

7.5.4 Kitchen utensils *(Track 150)*

No.	Cantonese Romanization	Chinese	Putonghua Romanization	English
1.	wok^6	鑊	guō 锅	wok
2.	zam^1 • baan^2	砧板	qiēcàibǎn 切菜板	cutting board
3.	faai^3 • zi^2	筷子	kuàizi 筷子	chopsticks
4.	caa^1	叉	chāzi 叉子	fork
5.	dou^1	刀	dāozi 刀子	knife
6.	dip^{2*}	碟	pánzi 盘子	plate
7.	seoi^2 • bou^1	水煲	shuǐhú 水壶	kettle
8.	din^6 faan^6 • bou^1	電飯煲	diànfànguō 电饭锅	electric rice cooker
9.	wun^2	碗	wǎn 碗	bowl
10.	gang^1	羹	tiáogēng 调羹	spoon

1 2 3 4 5 6

7.6 Exercise

7.6.1 Matching

1. jat^1 一 (　　) gu^1 • lou^1 • juk^6 咕嚕肉 *sweet & sour pork* — A. lung^4 籠
2. jat^1 一 (　　) din^6 • nou^5 電腦 *computer* — B. wun^2 碗
3. jat^1 一 (　　) tong^1 湯 *soup* — C. dip^6 碟
4. jat^1 一 (　　) gaa^3 • fe^1 咖啡 *coffee* — D. bou^6 部
5. jat^1 一 (　　) haa^1 • gaau^2 蝦餃 *shrimp dumplings* — E. bui^1 杯

7.6.2 Multiple choice

1. *Are you free?*

   Nei^5 你 ____________ haan^4 閒 aa^3 呀？

   A. haan^4 m^4 dak^1 閒唔得　　B. dak^1 得　　C. dak^1 m^4 dak^1 得唔得

2. *Dim sum is more delicious than hamburgers.*

   Dim^2 • sam^1 點心 hou^2 • sik^6 好食 ____________ hon^3 • bou^2 • baau^1 漢堡包。

   A. maai^4 埋　　B. gwo^3 過　　C. zo^2 咗

3. *I want to finish reading the book soon.*

   Ngo^5 我 soeng^2 想 faai^3 di^1 快啲 tai^2 睇 ____________ ni^1 bun^2 呢本 syu^1 書。

   A. maai^4 埋　　B. gwo^3 過　　C. hou^2 好

4. *He wants to earn more money.*

   Keoi^5 佢 soeng^2 想 wan^2 搵 ____________ cin^{2*} 錢。

   A. do^1 dim^2 多點　　B. dou^1 do^1 都多　　C. do^1 di^1 多啲

5. *Any time will be fine by me.*

   Ngo^5 我 ____________ dou^1 都 dak^1 得。

   A. gei^2 • si^4 幾時　　B. gei^2 • noi^6 幾耐　　C. gei^2 • do^1 幾多

7.6.3 Comprehension

Cin^4 • jat^6 ngo^5 joek^3 • zo^2 *(make appointments with)* loeng^5 go^3 pang^4 • jau^5 heoi^3 Zung^1 • waan^4 jam^2 • caa^4. Ziu^1 • zou^2 sap^6 dim^2 ngo^5 hai^2 Zung^1 • waan^4 dei^6 • tit^3 zaam^6 Hang^4 • sang^1 ngan^4 • hong^4 cin^4 • min^6 dang^2 keoi^5 • dei^6 sin^1.
前 日 我 約 咗 兩 個 朋 友 去 中 環 飲 茶 。 朝 早 十 點 我 喺 中 環 地 鐵 站 恒 生 銀 行 前 面 等 佢 哋 先 。

Gaa^1 • naam^4 sap^6 dim^2 lei^4 • zo^2, dang^2 • zo^2 hou^2 noi^6 Wing^6 • si^1 dou^1 mou^5 lei^4.
家 男 十 點 嚟 咗 ， 等 咗 好 耐 詠 詩 都 冇 嚟 。

Ngo^5 tung^4 Gaa^1 • naam^4 heoi^3 jat^1 gaan^1 zau^2 • lau^4 sik^6 dim^2 • sam^1. Go^2 • dou^6 ge^3 haa^1 • gaau^2 hou^2 leng^3, siu^1 • maai^{2*} dou^1 hou^2 hou^2 • sik^6.
我 同 家 男 去 一 間 酒 樓 食 點 心 。 嗰 度 嘅 蝦 餃 好 靚 ， 燒 賣 都 好 好 食 。

Sik^6 • baau^2 dim^2 • sam^1, ngo^5 • dei^6 maai^4 • daan^1, gan^1 • zyu^6 daap^3 din^6 • ce^1 heoi^3 Waan^1 • zai^2 tai^2 hei^3.
食 飽 點 心 ， 我 哋 埋 單 ， 跟 住 搭 電 車 去 灣 仔 睇 戲 。

Please answer the following questions:

1. *Q:* Ngo^5 joek^3 • zo^2 bin^1 • go^3 jam^2 • caa^4 aa^3?

   A: Ngo5 joek3 zo2 gaa1 naam4 tung4 wing6 si1

2. *Q:* Ngo^5 hai^2 bin^1 • dou^6 dang^2 keoi^5 • dei^6 sin^1 aa^3?

   A: Zung1 waan4 dei6 tit3 zaam6 Hang4 sang1 ngan4 hong4 cin4 min6

3. *Q:* Bin^1 • go^3 mou^5 lei^4 aa^3?

   A: wing6 si1

4. *Q:* Go^2 • dou^6 di^1 me^1 dim^2 • sam^1 hou^2 hou^2 • sik^6 aa^3?

   A: Haa1 gaau2

5. *Q:* Ngo^5 tung^4 Gaa^1 • naam^4 daap^3 me^1 ce^1 heoi^3 tai^2 hei^3 aa^3?

   A: din6 ce1

8

Kaa¹ • laa¹ • ou¹ • kei¹

卡拉 OK *Karaoke*

Learning Tasks

- to ask and talk about hobbies
- to ask and tell time frequency
- to ask for and indicate what to choose
- to list items

Grammar Notes

- time frequency:
  si⁴ • si⁴ • dou¹ 時時都 and jau⁵ • si⁴ 有時
- '*apart from…*':
  ceoi⁴ • zo² 除咗 … zung⁶ 仲 … tim¹ 添
- '*how often*' questions:
  gei² • noi⁶ 幾耐 … jat¹ ci³ 一次
- '*surprise / doubt*' questions : me¹ 咩
- '*when*' clauses: go² • zan⁶ • si²* 嗰陣時
- particle for listing items:
  … laa¹ 啦 , … laa¹ 啦 …
- alternative question '*A or B*': ding⁶ 定
- '*from A to B*': jau⁴ 由 … dou³ 到 …

Sounds and Tones

- Putonghua & Cantonese finals in comparison (2)

Supplementary Vocabulary

- activities
- meat and seafood
- vegetables
- fruit

Exercise

- matching
- multiple choice
- question and answer

 8.1 Vocabulary *(Track 151)*

No.	Cantonese Romanization	Cantonese Characters	Putonghua & Chinese Characters	English
1.	a) kei^{1} fong^{2*}	K 房	kǎ lā ok bāoxiāng 卡拉 ok 包厢	karaoke room
	b) ni^{1} gaan^{1} kei^{1} fong^{2*}	呢間 K 房	zhège kǎ lā ok bāoxiāng 这个卡拉 ok 包厢	this karaoke room
2.	syu^{1} • fuk^{6}	舒服	shūfu 舒服	comfortable
3.	jau^{5} • si^{4}	有時	yǒu shíhou 有时候	sometimes
4.	si^{4} • si^{4} dou^{1}	時時都	chángcháng 常常	always
5.	hoi^{1} *party*	開 party	kāi pàiduì 开派对	have a party
6.	a) coeng^{3} kei^{1}	唱 K	chàng kǎlāōukēi 唱卡拉 OK	sing karaoke
	b) coeng^{3} kaa^{1} • laa^{1} • ou^{1} • kei^{1}	唱卡拉OK	chàng kǎlāōukēi 唱卡拉 OK	sing karaoke
	c) coeng^{3} • gwo^{3} kaa^{1} • laa^{1} • ou^{1} • kei^{1}	唱過卡拉 OK	chàngguò kǎlāōukēi 唱过卡拉 OK	have sung karaoke
	d) mei^{6} coeng^{3} • gwo^{3}	未唱過	hái méiyǒu chàngguò 还没有唱过	have never sung (karaoke)
7.	ceoi^{4} • zo^{2}… zi^{1} • ngoi^{6}, zung^{6}…tim^{1}	除咗…之外，仲…添	chúle…yǐwài, hái 除了…以外，还	apart from…
8.	jyu^{4} • lok^{6}	娛樂	yúlè 娱乐	amusements
9.	daa^{2} maa^{4} • zoek^{2*}	打麻雀	dǎ májiàng 打麻将	play mahjong
10.	teng^{1} jin^{2} • coeng^{3} • wui^{2*}	聽演唱會	tīng yǎnchànghuì 听演唱会	attend a music concert
11.	…laa^{1}, …laa^{1}	…啦，…啦	…la, …la 啦，啦…	particle to list items
12.	…go^{2} • zan$^{}$ • si^{2*}	…嗰陣時	…de shíhou 的时候	when …
13.	jam^{2} be^{1} • zau^{2}	飲啤酒	hē píjiǔ 喝啤酒	drink beer
14.	zou^{6} wan^{6} • dung^{6}	做運動	zuò yùndòng 做运动	do sports

15.	daa^2 mong^5 • kau^4	打網球	dǎ wǎngqiú 打网球	play tennis
16.	hai^6 me^1	係咩	shì ma? 是吗	is that so
17.	mui^5 go^3 sing^1 • kei^4	每個星期	měi gè xīngqī 每个星期	every week
18.	a) ci^3	次	cì 次	time(s)
	b) gei^2 • noi^6 … jat^1 ci^3	幾耐⋯一次	duōjiǔ…yí cì 多久⋯一次	how often⋯once
	c) loeng^5 saam^1 ci^3	兩三次	liǎng sāncì 两三次	two to three times
	d) haa^6 ci^3	下次	xià cì 下次	next time
	e) coeng^3 • gwo^3 gei^2 ci^3	唱過幾次	chàngguo jǐ cì 唱过几次	have sung several times
19.	ceot^1 heoi^3 lo^2 di^1 je^5 sik^6 sin^1	出去攞啲嘢食先	xiān chūqù ná xiē chī de 先出去拿些吃的	go out and get some food first
20.	a) dim^2 go^1	點歌	diǎn gē 点歌	choose a song
	b) coeng^3 • go^1	唱歌	chàng gē 唱歌	sing a song
21.	a) … ding^6 …	定	háishì 还是	… or … (used in a question)
	b) waak^6 • ze^2	或者	huòzhě 或者	… or … (used in a statement)
22.	Gong^2 • sik^1	港式	Gǎngshì 港式	Hong Kong style
23.	sau^1 • fai^3	收費	shōufèi 收费	charge, cost
24.	jau^5 • peng^4-jau^5 • gwai^3	有平有貴	yǒu piányi de, yě yǒu guì de 有便宜的，也有貴的	some are cheap, some are expensive
25.	gaa^3 • cin^4	價錢	jiàqián 價錢	price, rate
26.	a) jau^4 … dou^3	由⋯到⋯	cóng 從 … dào 到 …	from … to …
	b) jau^4 sei^3 • sap^6 man^1 dou^3 ji^6 • baak^3 man^1 dou^1 jau^5	由四十蚊到二百蚊都有	cóng sì shí kuài dào èr bǎi kuài dōu yǒu 從四十塊到二百塊都有	range from forty to two hundred dollars
27.	zi^6 • zo^6 • caan^1	自助餐	zìzhùcān 自助餐	buffet

8.2 They are talking in a Karaoke restaurant. *(Track 152)*

Ni1 gaan1 kei1 fong2 hou2 syu1 • fuk6 aa3.
呢 間 K 房 好 舒 服 呀 。
This Karaoke room is comfortable.
这个卡拉OK包厢很舒服啊。

Nei5 • dei6 hai2 Hoeng1 • gong2 jau5 mou5 coeng3 • gwo3 kaa1 • laa1 • ou1 • kei1 aa3?
你 哋 喺 香 港 有 冇 唱 過 卡 拉 OK 呀 ？
Have you ever sung karaoke in Hong Kong?
你们在香港有没有唱过卡拉OK？

Jau5 aa3, ngo5 jau5 • si4 wui5 lei4 ni1 • dou6 hoi1 *party*.
有 呀 ， 我 有 時 會 嚟 呢 度 開 party 。
Yes, I have. Sometimes I have parties here.
对，我有时候会来这里开派对。

Ngo5 hai2 Hoeng1 • gong2 coeng3 • gwo3 gei2 ci3.
我 喺 香 港 唱 過 幾 次 。
I've sung (karaoke) several times in Hong Kong.
我在香港唱过几次。

Mou5 aa3, ngo5 mei6 coeng3 • gwo3.
冇 呀 ， 我 未 唱 過 。
No, I've never sung karaoke before.
没有，我没有唱过。

Gaa1 • man5, Hoeng1 • gong2 • jan4 ceoi4 • zo2 coeng3 kei1 zi1 • ngoi6, zung6 jau5 di1 me1 jyu4 • lok6 aa3?
嘉 敏 ， 香 港 人 除 咗 唱 K 之 外 ， 仲 有 啲 咩 娛 樂 呀 ？
Ka-Man, apart from karaoke, what kinds of amusements do Hong Kong people have?
嘉敏，香港人除了唱卡拉OK以外，还有些什么娱乐？

Maai5 • je5 laa1, daa2 maa4 • zoek2* laa1, teng1 jin2 • coeng3 • wui2* laa1.
買 嘢 啦 ， 打 麻 雀 啦 ， 聽 演 唱 會 啦 。
Shopping, playing mahjong, going to singing concerts....
买东西啦，打麻将啦，听演唱会啦…。

Nei5 • dei6 dak1 • haan4 go2 • zan6 • si2*, zung1 • ji3 zou6 me1 aa3?
你 哋 得 閒 嗰 陣 時 ， 鍾 意 做 咩 呀 ？
When you are free, what would you like to do?
你们有空的时候，喜欢做什么？

Ngo5 zung1 • ji3 tiu3 mou5 tung4 tai2 • hei3.
我 鍾 意 跳 舞 同 睇 戲 。
I like dancing and watching movies.
我喜欢跳舞和看电影。

Ngo5 zung1 • ji3 zou6 wan6 • dung6. Ceoi4 • zo2 paau2 bou6 zi1 • ngoi6, zung6 zung1 • ji3 daa2 mong5 • kau4 tim1!
我 鍾 意 做 運 動 。 除 咗 跑 步 之 外 ， 仲 鍾 意 打 網 球 添 ！
I like playing sports. Apart from jogging, I also like playing tennis.
我喜欢做运动。除了跑步以外，还喜欢打网球！

Ngo5 dou1 zung1 • ji3 daa2 mong5 • kau4.
我 都 鍾 意 網 球 打 網 球 。
I like playing tennis, too.
我也喜歡打网球。

Hai6 me1?
係 咩 ？
Is that so?
是嗎？

Nei5 gei2 • noi6 daa2 jat1 ci3 mong5 • kau4 aa3?
你 幾 耐 打 一 次 網 球 呀 ？
How often do you play tennis?
你多久打一次网球？？

Ngo5 mui5 go3 sing1 • kei4 dou1 wui5 daa2 loeng5 saam1 ci3.
我 每 個 星 期 都 會 打 兩 三 次 。
I play two to three times each week.
我每个星期都会打两三次。

Ngo5 • dei6 haa2 go3 sing1 • kei4 jat1 • cai4 daa2 mong5 • kau4, hou2 m4 hou2 aa3?
我 哋 下 個 星 期 一 齊 打 網 球 ， 好 唔 好 呀 ？
Let's play tennis next week, shall we?
我們下星期一起打网球，好不好？

M4 • hou2 • ji3 • si3, ngo5 haa6 • go3 sing1 • kei4 hou2 mong4, haa6 ci3 laa1.
唔 好 意 思 ， 我 下 個 星 期 好 忙 ， 下 次 啦 。
I'm sorry, I'll be very busy next week. Let's do it next time.
不好意思，下星期很忙，下次再说吧。

Nei5 • dei6 tou5 m4 tou5 • ngo6 aa3?
你哋肚唔肚餓呀？
Are you guys hungry?
你们饿了吗？

Ngo5 m4 tou5 • ngo6.
我唔肚餓。
I am not hungry.
我不饿。

Maa4 • maa2* • dei2*.
麻麻哋。
A little bit.
有点饿。

Ngo5 hou2 tou5 • ngo6, ceot1 heoi3 lo2 di1 je5 sik6 sin1. Nei5 • dei6 dim2 go1 laa1.
我好肚餓，出去攞啲嘢食先，你哋點歌啦。
I'm so hungry. I'll go out and get some food first. Why don't you guys choose songs!
我很饿，出去先拿些吃的。你们先点歌吧。

Nei5 • dei6 soeng2 coeng3 Gwong2 • dung1 go1 ding6 Jing1 • man4 go1 aa3?
你哋想唱廣東歌定英文歌呀？
Would you like to sing Cantonese songs or English ones?
你们想唱广东歌还是英文歌？

Ngo5 soeng2 coeng3 Jing1 • man4 go1.
我想唱英文歌。
I would like to sing English songs.
我想唱英文歌。

Jing1 • man4 go1 waak6 • ze2 Gwong2 • dung1 go1 dou1 dak1.
英文歌或者廣東歌都得。
Either English or Cantonese songs will do.
英文歌或者广东歌都行。

After eating and singing, they talk about Hong Kong-style karaoke

Gong2 • sik1 kaa1 • laa1 • ou1 • kei1 ge3 sau1 • fai3 gwai3 m4 gwai3 aa3?
港式卡拉OK嘅收費貴不貴呀？
Does Hong Kong-style karaoke cost a lot?
港式卡拉OK的收费贵不贵？

Jau5 • peng4 - jau5 • gwai3. Gaa3 • cin4 jau4 sei3 • sap6 man1 dou3 ji6 • baak3 man1 dou1 jau5.
有 平 有 貴 。 價 錢 由 四 十 蚊 到 二 百 蚊 都 有 。
Some are cheap, some are expensive. The fees range from forty to two hundred dollars.
有便宜的，也有贵的。价钱从四十块到二百块都有。

Gam1 • jat6 ngo5 • dei6 coeng3 kei1 tung4 sik6 zi6 • zo6 • caan1 jiu3 bei2 gei2 • do1 cin2* aa3?
今 日 我 哋 唱 K 同 食 自 助 餐 要 俾 幾 多 錢 呀 ？
How much do they charge for today's karaoke and the buffet?
今天我们唱卡拉OK跟吃自助餐要给多少钱呀？

Jat1 • baak3 saam1 • sap6 man1.
一 百 三 十 蚊 。
One hundred and thirty dollars.
一百三十块。

8.3 Grammar Notes

8.3.1 Time frequency : si4 • si4 • dou1 時時都 and jau4 • si4 有時 *(Track 153)*

"Si4 • si4 dou1 時時都" is always placed before the main verb or adjective to denote that something always or regularly happens. It is similar to Putonghua "常常".

P chángcháng 常常 + verb / adjective

'*Sometimes*' is expressed with "jau5 • si4 有時". It is also used when contrasting different actions or events at different times.

yǒu shíhou 有时候 + action / event

Examples:

1. Ngo5 si4 • si4 • dou1 zou6 wan6 • dung6.
   我 時 時 都 做 運 動 。
   I always play sports.
   我常常做运动。

2. Keoi5 jau5 • si4 coeng3 Jing1 • man4 • go1.
   佢 有 時 唱 英 文 本 歌 。
   She sometimes sings English songs.
   她有时候唱英文歌。

8.3.2 '*Apart from…*' : ceoi^{4} • zo^{2} 除咗 … zung^{6} 仲 … tim^{1} 添 *(Track 154)*

"Ceoi^{4} • zo^{2} 除咗 + X, zung^{6} 仲 + Y + tim^{1} 添" is used to highlight new information Y in addition to (ceoi^{4} • zo^{2}) the current information X. This pattern often ends with the sentence particle "tim^{1}" to add a feeling of unexpectedness. X can be a noun or verb phrase, and Y is always a verb phrase.

P chúle 除了 … hái 还

Examples:

1. Ngo^{5} ceoi^{4} • zo^{2} sik^{1} gong^{2} Gwong^{2} • dung^{1} • waa^{2*}, zung^{6} sik^{1} gong^{2} Pou^{2} • tung^{1} • waa^{2*} tim^{1}.
   我 除 咗 識 講 廣 東 話 ， 仲 識 講 普 通 話 添 。
   Apart from Cantonese, I can speak Putonghua as well.
   我除了会说广东话，还会说普通话。

2. Keoi^{5} ceoi^{4} • zo^{2} Bak^{1} • gik^{6}, zung^{6} heoi^{3} • gwo^{3} Naam^{4} • gik^{6} tim^{1}.
   佢 除 咗 北 極 ， 仲 去 過 南 極 添 。
   Other than the North Pole, he has also been to the South Pole.
   他除了北极，还去过南极。

8.3.3 '*How often*' questions : gei^{2} • noi^{6} 幾耐 … jat^{1} ci^{3} 一次 *(Track 155)*

"Gei^{2} • noi^{6} 幾耐 + verb + jat^{1} ci^{3} 一次 + object" is used to ask the frequency of an action concerned.

P duōjiǔ 多久 … yícì 一次

Examples:

1. *A:* Nei^{5} gei^{2} • noi^{6} heoi^{3} jat^{1} ci^{3} ciu^{1} • si^{5} aa^{3}?
   你 幾 耐 去 一 次 超 市 呀 ？
   How often do you go to supermarket?
   你多久去一次超级市场呀？

   B: Jat^{1} go^{3} sing^{1} • kei^{4} jat^{1} ci^{3}.
   一 個 星 期 一 次 。
   Once a week.
   一个星期一次。

2. *A:* Nei^{5} gei^{2} • noi^{6} zin^{2} jat^{1} ci^{3} tau^{4} • faat^{3} aa^{3}?
   你 幾 耐 剪 一 次 頭 髮 呀 ？
   How often do you get your hair cut?
   你多久剪一次头发？

   B: Loeng^{5} go^{3} jyut^{6}.
   兩 個 月 。
   Every two months.
   两个月。

8.3.4 '*Surprise/doubt*' questions : me^{1} 咩 *(Track 156)*

"Me^{1} 咩" is a question particle to express the speaker's surprise or doubt and check if it is really the case.

P ma 吗

Examples:

1. *A:* Jan^4 • jan^4 dou^1 m^4 heoi^3, nei^5 heoi^3 me^1?
人人都唔去，你去咩？
None of us will go. Are you really going?
人人都不去，你去吗？

B: Heoi^3.
去。
Yes, I'll go.
去。

2. *A:* Nei^5 m^4 • sai^2 ngo^5 faan^1 • jik^6 me^1?
你唔駛我翻譯咩？
Do you really not need me to translate it for you?
你不用我翻译吗？

B: Jiu^3 aa^3.
要呀。
Yes, I do.
我需要。

8.3.5 '*When...*' clauses : go^2 • zan^6 • si^{2*} 嗰陣時 (Track 157)

In the pattern "X + go^2 • zan^6 • si^{2*} 嗰陣時, Y", X denotes the time when Y occurs. Unlike the '*when*' clause in English, "X + go^2 • zan^6 • si^{2*} 嗰陣時" is always used before Y.

P … de shíhou 的时候

Examples:

1. Nei^5 dak^1 • haan^4 go^2 • zan^6 • si^{2*}, jat^1 • cai^4 tai^2 • hei^3 laa^1.
你得閒嗰陣時一齊睇戲啦。
When you have time, let's watch a movie together.
你有空的时候一起看电影吧。

2. Ngo^5 jau^5 • cin^{2*} go^2 • zan^6 • si^{2*}, zung^1 • ji^3 maai^5 • je^5.
我有錢嗰陣時鍾意買嘢。
I like shopping when I have money.
我有钱的时候喜欢买东西。

8.3.6 Particle for listing items : … laa^1 啦 , … laa^1 啦 … (Track 158)

To list items, simply put the particle "laa^1 啦" after each item.

P … la, … la …
…啦，…啦

Examples:

1. Jau^4 • seoi^2 laa^1, daa^2 laam^4 • kau^4 laa^1, daa^2 mong^5 • kau^4 laa^1, ngo^5 dou^1 zung^1 • ji^3 gaa^3.
游水啦、打籃球啦、打網球啦，我都鍾意㗎。
Swimming, playing basketball, playing tennis and so on are all my favorites.
游泳啦、打篮球啦、打网球啦，我都喜欢的。

2. Haa^1 • gaau^2 laa^1, siu^1 • maai^{2*} laa^1, ceon^1 • gyun^2 laa^1, dou^1 hou^2 hou^2 • sik^6.
蝦 餃 啦 、 燒 賣 啦 、 春 卷 啦 ， 都 好 好 食 。
Shrimp dumplings, pork dumplings, spring rolls and the others are all delicious.
虾饺啦、烧卖啦、春卷啦，都很好吃。

8.3.7 Alternative questions '*A or B*': ding^6 定 *(Track 159)*

"A ding^6 B" is used when asking someone to make a choice between A and B.

P … A háishì 还是 B

Examples:

1. *A:* Nei^5 zung^1 • ji^3 jam^2 gaa^3 • fe^1 ding^6 caa^4 aa^3?
你 鍾 意 飲 咖 啡 定 茶 呀 ？
Would you like to have coffee or tea?
你喜欢喝咖啡还是茶？

B: Gaa^3 • fe^1.
咖 啡 。
Coffee.
咖啡。

2. *A:* Nei^5 soeng^2 gong^2 Gwong^2 • dung^1 • waa^2 ding^6 Jing^1 • man^{2*} aa^3?
你 想 講 廣 東 話 定 英 文 呀 ？
Do you want to speak Cantonese or English?
你想说广东还是英文呢？

B: Jing^1 • man^{2*}.
英 文 。
English.
英文。

8.3.8 '*From A to B*': jau^4 由 … dou^3 到 … *(Track 160)*

"Jau^4 由 + A + dou^3 到 + B" means '*from A to B*', expressing the range of price, duration, distance, etc. When expressing the action involved, the verb is placed between "jau^4 由 + A" and "dou^3 到 + B".

P cóng 从 + A + dào 到 + B

Examples:

1. Ngo^5 gam^4 • jat^6 jau^4 ziu^1 • zou^2 soeng^5 tong^5 soeng^5 • dou^3 je^6 • maan^5 .
我 今 日 由 朝 早 上 堂 上 到 夜 晚 。
Today I have classes from morning to night.
我今天从早上上课上到晚上。

2. *A:* Jau^4 Saa^1 • tin^4 dou^3 Wong^6 • gok^3 jiu^3 gei^2 • noi^6 aa^3?
由 沙 田 到 旺 角 要 幾 耐 呀 ？
How long does it take from Sha Tin to Mong Kok?
我从沙田到旺角要多久呢？

B: Jat^1 go^3 zung^1 • tau^4.
一 個 鐘 頭 。
One hour.
一小时。

8.4 Cantonese and Putonghua finals in comparison (1) :

Some finals in Putonghua and Cantonese are spelt alike as well as sound alike. *(Track 161)*

Putonghua	Chinese characters	Cantonese
yī	衣	ji^{1}
gū	菇	gu^{1}
yú	魚	jyu^{2*}

Putonghua	Chinese characters	Cantonese
fēi	飛	fei^{1}
dōu	都	dou^{1}

The following four finals are spelt alike in Putonghua and Cantonese, but the actual sound values are different. Listen carefully and try to recognize the differences. *(Track 162)*

chē	車	ce^{1}
qīng	清	cing^{1}

huī	灰	fui^{1}
zhèng	鄭	zeng^{6}

There is also a case where the same sound value is spelt differently in Putonghua and Cantonese. *(Track 163)*

mā	媽	maa^{1}

dōng	東	dung^{1}

Some Cantonese finals sound very different from those in Putonghua. The table below displays some frequently used Putonghua finals on the left and their Cantonese counterparts on the right for your comparison: *(Track 164)*

Putonghua	Chinese characters	Cantonese
dà	大	daai^{6}
jiā	加	gaa^{1}
jiā	佳	gaai^{1}
kē	科	fo^{1}
jiè	借	ze^{3}
xì	戲	hei^{3}
jī	雞	gai^{1}
èr	二	ji^{6}
shū	書	syu^{1}
xū	需	seoi^{1}

Putonghua	Chinese characters	Cantonese
ài	愛	oi^{3}
bēi	杯	bui^{1}
duì	對	deoi^{3}
guì	貴	gwai^{3}
bāo	包	baau^{1}
gāo	高	gou^{1}
gòu	夠	gau^{3}
qiū	秋	cau^{1}
jiào	教	gaau^{3}
xiào	笑	siu^{3}

8.5 Supplementary Vocabulary

8.5.1 Activities *(Track 165)*

No.	Cantonese Romanization	Chinese	Putonghua Romanization	English
1.	king^{1} • gai^{2}	傾偈	liáotiānr 聊天儿	chatting
2.	jaai^{2} daan^{1} • ce^{1}	踹單車	qí zìxíngchē 骑自行车	cycling
3.	haang^{4} • saan^{1}	行山	pá shān 爬山	hiking
4.	paau^{2} • bou^{6}	跑步	pǎo bù 跑步	jogging
5.	teng^{1} jam^{1} • ngok^{6}	聽音樂	tīng yīnyuè 听音乐	listening to music
6.	daa^{2} laam^{4} • kau^{4}	打籃球	dǎ lánqiú 打篮球	playing basketball
7.	daa^{2} • gei^{1}	打機	wánr yóuxì jī 玩儿游戏机	playing computer games
8.	jau^{4} • seoi^{2}	游水	yóuyǒng 游泳	swimming
9.	jing^{2} • soeng^{2}*	影相	zhào xiàng 照相	taking photos
10.	tai^{2} • hei^{3}	睇戲	kàn diànyǐng 看电影	watching movies

8.5.2 Meat and seafood *(Track 166)*

No.	Cantonese Romanization	Chinese	Putonghua Romanization	English
1.	ngau^{4} • juk^{6}	牛肉	niúròu 牛肉	beef
2.	gai^{1}	雞	jī 鸡	chicken
3.	haai^{5}	蟹	pángxiè 螃蟹	crab
4.	aap^{3}	鴨	yā 鸭	duck
5.	jyu^{2}*	魚	yú 鱼	fish
6.	joeng^{4} • juk^{6}	羊肉	yángròu 羊肉	mutton
7.	hou^{4}	蠔	mǔlì 牡蛎	oyster
8.	zyu^{1} • juk^{6}	豬肉	zhū ròu 猪肉	pork
9.	daai^{3} • zi^{2}	帶子	yuán bèi 元贝	scallop
10.	haa^{1}	蝦	xiā 虾	shrimp

8.5.3 Vegetables *(Track 167)*

No.	Cantonese Romanization	Chinese	Putonghua Romanization	English
1.	lou^6 • seon^2	蘆筍	lúsǔn 芦笋	asparagus
2.	cung^1	蔥	cōng 葱	spring onions
3.	fu^2 • gwaa^1	苦瓜	kǔguā 苦瓜	bitter melon
4.	je^4 • coi^3	椰菜	juǎnxīncài 卷心菜	cabbage
5.	gaai^3 • laan^2	芥蘭	jiè lán 芥兰	Chinese kale
6.	baak^6 • coi^3	白菜	báicài 白菜	Chinese white cabbage
7.	ai^2 • gwaa^1	矮瓜	qiézi 茄子	eggplant
8.	saang^1 • coi^3	生菜	shēngcài 生菜	lettuce
9.	bo^1 • coi^3	菠菜	bōcài 菠菜	spinach
10.	dung^1 • gwaa^1	冬瓜	dōngguā 冬瓜	winter melon

8.5.4 Fruit *(Track 168)*

No.	Cantonese Romanization	Chinese	Putonghua Romanization	English
1.	ping^4 • gwo^2	蘋果	píngguǒ 苹果	apple
2.	hoeng^1 • ziu^1	香蕉	xiāngjiāo 香蕉	banana
3.	ce^1 • lei^4 • zi^2	車厘子	yīngtáo 樱桃	cherry
4.	sai^1 • jau^2	西柚	yòuzi 柚子	grapefruit
5.	tai^4 • zi^2	提子	pútao 葡萄	grapes
6.	mong^1 • gwo^2	芒果	mángguǒ 芒果	mango
7.	caang^2	橙	júzi 橘子	orange
8.	muk^6 • gwaa^1	木瓜	mùguā 木瓜	papaya
9.	bo^1 • lo^4	菠蘿	fènglí 凤梨	pineapple
10.	si^6 • do^1 • be^1 • lei^2*	士多啤梨	cǎoméi 草莓	strawberry

8.6 Exercise

8.6.1 Matching

1. tai^{2} din^{6} • si^{6} 睇電視	C	A. reading
2. teng^{1} jam^{1} • ngok^{6} 聽音樂	E	B. running
3. tai^{2} • syu^{1} 睇書	A	C. watching TV
4. paau^{2} • bou^{6} 跑步	B	D. singing
5. coeng^{3} • go^{1} 唱歌	D	E. listening to music

8.6.2 Multiple choice

1. *I sometimes play tennis.*

   Ngo^{5} 我 __________ daa^{2} mong^{5} • kau^{4} 打網球。

   A. si^{4} • si^{4} • dou^{1} 時時都　　B. jau^{5} • si^{4} 有時　　C. gei^{2} • si^{4} 幾時

2. *Apart from English, I can speak French as well.*

   Ngo^{5} 我 __________ sik^{1} 識 gong^{1} 講 jing^{1} • man^{2*} 英文，__________ sik^{1} 識 gong^{1} 講 Faat^{3} • man^{2*} 法文 tim^{1} 添。

   A. ceoi^{4} • zo^{2} 除咗 … dou^{3} 到　　B. ceoi^{4} • zo^{2} 除咗 … zung^{6} 仲　　C. jau^{4} 由 … dou^{3} 到

3. *Do you like to eat Chinese food or Western food.*

   Nei^{5} 你 zung^{1} • ji^{3} 鍾意 sik^{6} 食 Zung^{1} • caan^{1} 中餐 __________ Sai^{1} • caan^{1} 西餐 aa^{3} 呀？

   A. ding^{6} 定　　B. gwo^{3} 過　　C. baau^{2} 飽

4. *I like to travel when I have time.*

   Ngo^{5} 我 jau^{5} 有 si^{4} • gaan^{3} 時間 __________ zung^{1} • ji^{3} 鍾意 heoi^{3} 去 leoi^{5} • hang^{4} 旅行。

   A. gei^{2} • si^{4} 幾時　　B. gei^{2} • noi^{6} 幾耐　　C. go^{2} • zan^{6} • si^{2*} 嗰陣時

5. *How often do you go to the library?*

   Nei^{5} 你 __________ heoi^{3} 去 jat^{1} ci^{3} 一次 tou^{4} • syu^{1} • gun^{2} 圖書館 aa^{3} 呀？

   A. gei^{2} • si^{4} 幾時　　B. gei^{2} • noi^{6} 幾耐　　C. gei^{2} • do^{1} 幾多

8.6.3 Question and answer

	Peter	*Mary*	*Jane*	*Paul*	*You*
do exercise	✓	✓	✗	✗	
watch movies	✗	✗	✓	✗	
go shopping	✗	✓	✗	✗	
surf the net	✓	✗	✗	✗	

Please answer the following questions:

1. *Q:* *Jane* zung1 m4 zung1 • ji3 tai2 hei3 • aa3 ?

   A: ____________________

2. *Q:* Bin1 • go3 zung1 • ji3 zou6 wan6 • dung6 tung4 soeng5 • mong5 aa3 ?

   A: ____________________

3. *Q:* *Mary* jau5 di1 me1 jyu4 • lok6 aa3 ?

   A: ____________________

4. *Q:* Bin1 • go3 me1 jyu4 • lok6 dou1 m4 zung1 • ji3 aa3 ?

   A: ____________________

5. *Q:* Nei5 dak1 • haan4 zung1 • ji3 zou6 di1 me1 aa3 ?

   A: ____________________

9 M^4 syu^1 • fuk^6

唔舒服 *Not feeling well*

Learning Tasks

- to ask and indicate if someone needs to do something or not
- to understand what people say in the clinic
- to tell the reasons behind illnesses
- to indicate the symptoms of illnesses
- to ask about the characteristics of the four seasons in Hong Kong
- to talk about common terms to describe weather

Grammar Notes

- necessity questions '*isn't it necessary to...*' : sai^2 m^4 • sai^2 駛唔駛
- '*because... (therefore)...*' : jan^1 • wai^6 因為 … so^2 • ji^5 所以
- two types of relative clauses
- superlative degree '*most*' : zeoi^3 最
- '*A is not so + adjective as B*' : mou^5 gam^3 冇咁
- '*although...*' : seoi^1 • jin^4 雖然 … daan^6 • hai^6 但係
- final particle for '*certainties*' : gaa^3 laa^3 㗎喇
- final particle for '*only*' : ze^1 啫

Sounds and Tones

- Putonghua and Cantonese final (2)'s cross-referential practice

Supplementary Vocabulary

- human body
- minor illnesses
- medicine treatment
- weather

Exercise

- matching
- multiple choice
- translation

9.1 Vocabulary *(Track 169)*

No.	Cantonese Romanization	Cantonese Characters	Putonghua & Chinese Characters	English
1.	soeng2 tai2 ji1 • sang1	想睇醫生	xiǎng kàn yīshēng 想看医生	want to see the doctor
2.	jyu6 • joek3	預約	yùyuē 预约	advance booking
3.	a) sai2 m4 sai2	駛唔駛	xūyào bù xūyào 需要不需要	is it necessary
	b) m4 • sai2	唔駛	bù xūyào 不需要	not necessary
	c) jiu3	要	xūyào 需要	necessary
4.	taam3 jit6	探熱	liáng tǐwēn 量体温	measure body temperature
5.	dak1 gaa3 laa3	得㗎喇	xíng le 行了	done / okay
6.	dang2 jat1 • zan6	等一陣	děng yíxià 等一下	wait for a moment
7.	beng6 • zo2	病咗	shēngbìng 生病	become sick
8.	daa2 hat1 • ci1	打乞嗤	dǎ pēntì 打喷嚏	sneeze
9.	tau4 • tung3	頭痛	tóuténg 头疼	headache
10.	faat3 • siu1	發燒	fā shāo 发烧	fever
11.	lau4 bei6 • tai3	流鼻涕	liú bítì 流鼻涕	running nose
12.	hau4 • lung4 tung3	喉嚨痛	hóulóngtòng 喉咙痛	sore throat
13.	a) soeng1 • fung1	傷風	xiǎo gǎnmào 小感冒	catch cold
	b) gam2 • mou6	感冒	gǎnmào 感冒	have a flu
14.	laang5 • hei3 taai3 dung3	冷氣太凍	kōngtiáo tài lěng 空调太冷	air condition is too cold
15.	jan1 • wai6 … so2 • ji5 …	因為…所以	yīnwèi…suǒyǐ… 因为… 所以	because … , therefore
16.	sik6 • co3 je5	食錯嘢	chīcuò dōngxi 吃错东西	get a reaction after eating food
17.	gam2	咁	zhème, nàme 这么、那么	so

18.	a) je5 • sik6	嘢食	shíwù 食物	food
	b) di1 je5 • sik6 hou2 jung4 • ji6 bin3 • waai6	啲嘢食好容易變壞	shíwù hěn róngyi biànhuài 食物很容易变坏	The food easily goes bad.
19.	a) zaap6 • gwaan3	習慣	xíguàn 习惯	be used to
	b) m4 zaap6 • gwaan3	唔習慣	bù xíguàn 不习惯	not used to
	c) zaap6 m4 zaap6 • gwaan3	習唔習慣	xíguàn bù xíguàn 习惯不习惯	are you used to…?
20.	mou5 gam3	冇咁…	méiyou nàme… 没有那么…	not so …as
21.	jat1 nin4 sei3 • gwai3	一年四季	yì nián sìjì 一年四季	four seasons in a year
22.	a) gwai3 • zit3	季節	jìjié 季节	season
	b) zung1 • ji3 bin1 • go3 gwai3 • zit3	鍾意邊個季節	xǐhuan nǎ yí ge jìjié 喜欢哪一个季节	which season do you like
23.	ceon1 • tin1	春天	chūntiān 春天	spring
24.	nyun5	暖	nuǎnhuo 暖和	warm
25.	sap1	濕	cháoshī 潮湿	humid
26.	haa6 • tin1	夏天	xiàtiān 夏天	summer
27.	jit6	熱	rè 热	hot
28.	cau1 • tin1	秋天	qiūtiān 秋天	autumn
29.	loeng4 • song2	涼爽	liángkuai 凉快	cool
30.	dung1 • tin1	冬天	dōngtiān 冬天	winter
31.	dung3	凍	lěng 冷	cold
32.	zeoi3	最	zuì 最	most
33.	seoi1 • jin4… , daan6 • hai6 …	雖然…但係…	suīrán 虽然… dànshì 但是…	although … , …
34.	dai6 • jat6 zoi3 king1	第日再傾	gǎitiān zài liáo 改天再聊	talk to you later
35.	ze1	啫	éryǐ 而已	final particle to denote just

36.	sik^{6} di^{1} joek^{6}	食啲藥	chī diǎnr yào 吃点儿药	take some medicine
37.	hou^{2} • faan^{1}	好返	quányù 痊愈	recover from illness

9.2 Tai-Lung and Ka-Man meet at the school clinic. *(Track 170)*

At the reception desk

Ngo^{5} soeng^{2} tai^{2} ji^{1} • sang^{1}.
我 想 睇 醫 生 。
I want to see a doctor.
我想看医生。

Jau^{5} mou^{5} jyu^{6} • joek^{3} aa^{3}?
有 冇 預 約 呀 ？
Do you have an appointment?
有没有预约？

Mou^{5} aa^{3}.
冇 呀 。
No.
没有。

Sai^{2} m^{4} sai^{2} taam^{3} • jit^{6} aa^{3}?
駛 唔 駛 探 熱 呀 ？
Do you need your temperature taken?
需要量体温吗？

Jiu^{3} aa^{3}, m^{4} • goi^{1}.
要 呀 ， 唔 該 。
Yes, please.
需要，谢谢。

Dak^{1} gaa^{3} laa^{3}, dang^{2} jat^{1} • zan^{6} laa^{1}.
得 㗎 喇 ， 等 一 陣 啦 。
Alright. Please wait for a moment.
行了，等一下吧。 。

M^{4} • goi^{1}.
唔 該 。
Thank you.
谢谢。

Tai-Lung sees Ka-Man waiting in the clinic.

Gaa1 • man5, nei5 dou1 beng6 • zo2 aa4?
嘉敏，你都病咗嗬？
Ka-Man, are you sick, too?
嘉敏，你也生病了？

Hai6 aa3, kam4 • maan5 daap3 go2 gaa3 baa1 • si2* ge3 laang5 • hei3 taai3 dung3, so2 • ji5 m4 syu1 • fuk6. Gam2, nei5 ne1?
係呀，琴晚搭嗰架巴士嘅冷氣太凍，所以唔舒服。噉，你呢？
Yes, the bus I took last night was too cold, so I caught a cold afterwards. How about you?
是，昨天晚上坐的那辆公交车的空调太冷，所以不舒服了。那，你呢？

Jan1 • wai6 sik6 • co3 je5, so2 • ji5 m4 syu1 • fuk6.
因為食錯嘢，所以唔舒服。
I must've ate something wrong, so I feel uncomfortable.
因为吃错东西，所以不舒服。

Ji4 • gaa1 gam3 jit6, di1 je5 • sik6 hou2 jung4 • ji6 bin3 • waai6 gaa3!
而家咁熱，啲嘢食好容易變壞㗎！
It's so hot now, so the food goes bad so easily.
现在这么热，食物很容易变坏啊！

Ngo5 zan1 • hai6 hou2 m4 zaap6 • gwaan3 Hoeng1 • gong2 ge3 haa6 • tin1. Cau1 • tin1 gei2 • si4 lei4 aa3?
我真係好唔習慣香港嘅夏天。秋天幾時嚟呀？
I really can't get used to the summer in Hong Kong. When will autumn come?
我真的很不习惯香港的夏天。秋天什么时候来？

Sap6 • jyut6 zau6 mou5 gam3 jit6 laa3.
十月就冇咁熱喇。
It will be not as hot in October.
十月就没有那么热了。

Hoeng1 • gong2 jat1 nin4 sei3 • gwai3, cau1 • tin1 hai6 m4 hai6 zeoi3 syu1 • fuk6 aa3?
香港一年四季，秋天係唔係最舒服呀？
Among the four seasons in a year, autumn is the most comfortable season, isn't it?
香港一年四季，秋天最舒服吗？

Hai^{6} aa^{3}, cau^{1} • tin^{1} zeoi^{3} syu^{1} • fuk^{6} gaa^{3} laa^{3}.
係 呀 ， 秋 天 最 舒 服 㗎 喇 。
Yes, autumn is the most comfortable.
对，秋天最舒服了。

Ceon^{1} • tin^{1} hai^{6} m^{4} hai^{6} dou^{1} hou^{2} syu^{1} • fuk^{6} aa^{3}?
春 天 係 唔 係 都 好 舒 服 呀 ？
Is spring also comfortable?
春天也很舒服吗？

Hai^{6} zau^{6} hai^{6}! Seoi^{1} • jin^{4} ceon^{1} • tin^{1} hou^{2} nyun^{5}, daan^{6} • hai^{6} hou^{2} sap^{1}.
係 就 係 ！ 雖 然 春 天 好 暖 ， 但 係 好 濕 。
Right, spring is warm, but it's very humid.
是就是！虽然春天很温暖，但是十分潮湿。

Gam^{2}, Hoeng^{1} • gong^{2} ge^{3} dung^{1} • tin^{1} dung^{3} m^{4} dung^{3} aa^{3}?
噉 ， 香 港 嘅 冬 天 凍 唔 凍 呀 ？
Then, is Hong Kong cold during winter?
那，香港的冬天冷吗？

Dung^{1} • tin^{1} m^{4} hai^{6} hou^{2} dung^{3}.
冬 天 唔 係 好 凍 。
Winter is not so cold.
冬天不是很冷。

The nurse asks Ka-Man to go into examination room

Can^{4} Gaa^{1} • man^{5}.
陳 嘉 敏 。
Chan Ka-Man.
陈嘉敏。

Ngo^{5} jiu^{3} tai^{2} ji^{1} • saang^{1}, dai^{6} • jat^{6} zoi^{3} king^{1} laa^{1}.
我 要 睇 醫 生 ， 第 日 再 傾 啦 。
I must see a doctor. Talk to you later.
我要看医生，改天再聊吧。

In the examination room

Nei^{5} bin^{1} • dou^{6} m^{4} syu^{1} • fuk^{6} aa^{3}?
你 邊 度 唔 舒 服 呀 ？
What are your symptoms?
你哪里不舒服？

Daa2 hat1 • ci1, tau4 • tung3.
打乞嗤、頭痛。
I have been sneezing and a headache.
打喷嚏、头疼。

The doctor checks the body temperature result.

Mou5 faat3 • siu1.
有發燒。
You don't have a fever.
没有发烧。

Jau5 mou5 lau4 bei6 • tai3, hau4 • lung4 tung3 aa3?
有冇流鼻涕、喉嚨痛呀？
Do you have a runny nose or a sore throat?
有没有流鼻涕、喉咙疼？

Jau5 lau4 bei6 • tai3, dou1 jau5 hau4 • lung4 tung3.
有流鼻涕，都有喉嚨痛。
I have a runny nose as well as a sore throat.
有点鼻涕、有点喉咙疼。

Soeng1 • fung1 ze1, sik6 di1 joek6 zau6 hou2 • faan1 gaa3 laa3.
傷風啫，食啲藥就好返㗎喇。
You just caught a cold. Take some medicine and you will get well.
小感冒而已，吃点药就痊愈了。

9.3 Grammar Notes

9.3.1 Necessity questions '*isn't it necessary to…*': sai2 m4 • sai2 駛唔駛 *(Track 171)*

"Sai2 m4 sai2 駛唔駛…？" is used to ask whether something is necessary or not. It is similar to Putonghua "需要…嗎". Sometimes it is also used when offering help as in example 2.

To answer yes, "jiu3 要" is used, while no is expressed with "m4 sai2 唔駛".

P xūyào 需要… ma 吗？

Examples:

1. *A:* Sai[2] m[4] • sai[2] sau[1] cin[2*] aa[3]?
駛 唔 駛 收 錢 呀 ？
Do you charge money for this?
需要付钱吗？

B: Jiu[3] aa[3].
要 呀 。
Yes.
要的。

2. *A:* Sai[2] m[4] • sai[2] bong[1] sau[2] aa[3]?
駛 唔 駛 幫 手 呀 ？
Do you need my help?
需要我帮忙吗？

B: M[4] • sai[2] laa[3], m[4] • goi[1].
唔 駛 喇 ， 唔 該 。
No, thank you.
不用了，谢谢。

9.3.2 '*Because… therefore…*': jan[1] • wai[6] 因為 … so[2] • ji[5] 所以 (Track 172)

The clause expressing reason begins with "jan[1] • wai[6] 因為" (*because*), and the main clause is preceded by "so[2] • ji[5] 所以" (*so, therefore*). These are one of parallel clauses in Cantonese, so both "jan[1] • wai[6]" and "so[2] • ji[5]" typically appear concurrently, although one of them can be omitted. The "jan[1] • wai[6]" clause typically comes before the "so[2] • ji[5]" clause.

P yīnwèi 因为 …
suǒyǐ 所以

Examples:

1. Jan[1] • wai[6] ngo[5] m[4] syu[1] • fuk[6], so[2] • ji[5] m[4] lei[4] dak[1].
因 為 我 唔 舒 服 ， 所 以 唔 嚟 得 。
Because I am feeling unwell, I cannot come.
因为我不舒服，所以不能来。

2. Jan[1] • wai[6] keoi[5] hou[2] leng[3], so[2] • ji[5] jan[4] • jan[4] dou[1] zung[1] • ji[3] keoi[5].
因 為 佢 好 靚 ， 所 以 人 人 都 鍾 意 佢 。
Because she is very pretty, everyone likes her.
因为她很漂亮，所以每个人都喜欢她。

9.3.3 Two types of relative clauses (Track 173)

The relative clause in Cantonese can be expressed in two ways in Cantonese: One is "relative clause + ge[3] 嘅 + noun" as in example 1; the other is "relative clause + ni[1] 呢 / go[2] 嗰 + classifier + noun" as in example 2. Note that English takes the reverse order: "noun + *that* / *which* / *who* + relative clause".

P … de 的 …

Examples:

1. Haang^{4} • gan^{2} • lei^{4} ge^{3} jan^{4} hai^{6} ngo^{5} tung^{4} • fong^{2*}.
   行 緊 嚟 嘅 人 係 我 同 房 。
   The person coming along is my roommate.
   正走过来的是我室友。

2. Ngo^{5} kam^{4} • jat^{6} tai^{2} go^{2} ceot^{1} hei^{3} hou^{2} hou^{2} • siu^{3}.
   我 琴 日 睇 嗰 齣 戲 好 好 笑 。
   The film I saw yesterday was very funny.
   我昨天看的那部电影很可笑。

9.3.4 Superlative degree '*most*': zeoi^{3} 最 (Track 174)

"Zeoi^{3} 最 + adjective" is used to show the superlative degree.

P zuì 最

Examples:

1. Nei^{5} zeoi^{3} hou^{2} • jan^{4}.
   你 最 好 人 。
   You are the greatest person.
   你这个人最好。

2. Ngo^{5} zeoi^{3} zung^{1} • ji^{3} jau^{4} • seoi^{2}.
   我 最 鍾 意 游 水 。
   I like swimming most.
   我最喜欢游泳。

9.3.5 '*A is not so + adjective + as B*': A mou^{5} 冇 + B + gam^{3} 咁 + adjective (Track 175)

"Mou^{5} 冇 + B + gam^{3} 咁 + adjective" is used to express something (*A*) is '*not so + adjective + as B*'. When the object of comparison is understood from the context, B can be omitted as in example 2.

P méiyǒu … nàme 沒有…那麼

Examples:

1. Keoi^{5} mou^{5} nei^{5} gam^{3} cung^{1} • ming^{4}.
   佢 冇 你 咁 聰 明 。
   He is not as clever as you are.
   他没有你那么聪明。

2. Gam1 • jat6 mou5 gam3 jit6.
   今 日 冇 咁 熱 。
   Today is not so hot.
   今天没有那么热。

9.3.6 *'Although … …'*: seoi1 • jin4 雖然 … daan6 • hai6 但係 (Track 176)

"Seoi1 • jin4 雖然 + X , daan6 • hai6 但係 + Y" is used to express "*although X, Y*". Like other parallel clauses, both X and Y are often marked concurrently by conjunctions, although it is possible to omit either "seoi1 • jin4" or "daan6 • hai6".

P suīrán … dànshì …
虽然… 但是…

Examples:

1. Seoi1 • jin4 ji4 • gaa1 hai6 haa6 • tin1, daan6 • hai6 zung6 • jau5 di1 Hoeng1 • gong2 • jan4 zung1 • ji3 daa2 • bin1 • lou4.
   雖 然 而 家 係 夏 天 ， 但 係 仲 有 啲 香 港 人 鍾 意 打 邊 爐 。
   Although it's summer right now, some Hong Kong people like to eat hot pot.
   虽然现在是夏天，但是还有些香港人喜欢吃火锅。

2. Seoi1 • jin4 ngo5 ge3 Gwong2 • dung1 • waa2* maa4 maa2* dei2*, daan6 • hai6 ngo5 jau5 hou2 do1 Hoeng1 • gong2 pang4 • jau5.
   雖 然 我 嘅 廣 東 話 麻 麻 哋 ， 但 係 我 有 好 多 香 港 朋 友 。
   My Cantonese is not very good, but I have many Hong Kong friends.
   虽然我的广东话不大好，但是我有很多香港朋友。

9.3.7 Final particle to show *'certainties'*: … gaa3 laa3 㗎喇 (Track 177)

"… gaa3 laa3 㗎喇" is a double final particle to show certainties such as the speaker's confidence or firm determination.

P similar to the sentence particle "de 的"

Examples:

1. Dak1 gaa3 laa3, mou5 man6 • tai4 gaa3 laa3.
   得 㗎 喇 ， 冇 問 題 㗎 喇 。
   It's okay, that should be no problem.
   行，没有问题的。

2. Ngo5 jat1 • ding6 bei2 • faan1 nei5 gaa3 laa3.
   我 一 定 俾 返 你 㗎 喇 。
   I'll surely return it to you.
   我一定会还给你的。

9.3.8 Final particle to show '*only*': … ze[1] 啫 *(Track 178)*

"Ze[1] 啫" is a sentence final particle to add the meaning of '*only*', limiting the scope expressed by the number or a degree adverb.

P …éryǐ …而已

Examples:

1. Ngo[5] lei[4] • zo[2] Hoeng[1] • gong[2] gei[2] go[3] jyut[6] ze[1].
   我 嚟 咗 香 港 幾 個 月 啫 。
   It's been only a few months since I came to Hong Kong.
   我来了香港几个月而已。

2. Ngo[5] sik[1] gong[2] siu[2] • siu[2] Gwong[2] • dung[1] • waa[2]* ze[1].
   我 識 講 少 少 廣 東 話 啫 。
   I can only speak a little Cantonese .
   我会说一点广东话而已。

9.4 Cantonese and Putonghua finals in comparison (2) :

In this section, we will see how Cantonese finals with -m / -n / -ng and -p / -t / -k endings are related to Putonghua finals.

Putonghua '-n' sometimes corresponds to Cantonese '-n', but sometimes '-m'. Putonghua '-an' often corresponds to Cantonese '-aan / -aam', while '-en / -in' corresponds to '-an / -am'.
(Track 179)

Putonghua	Chinese characters	Cantonese	Putonghua	Chinese characters	Cantonese
fān	翻	faan¹	fēn	分	fan¹
sān	三	saam¹	xīn	新	san¹
zhàn	站	zaam⁶	jìn	浸	zam³

Putonghua '-ian' corresponds to Cantonese '-in' or '-im'. *(Track 180)*

tiān	天	tin¹	jiān	尖	zim¹
miàn	面	min⁶	diǎn	點	dim²

Putonghua '-ang' corresponds to Cantonese '-ong', while Putonghua '-iang' and '(zh / ch / sh) -ang' correspond to Cantonese '-oeng'. *(Track 181)*

làng	浪	long⁶	dāng	當	dong¹
xiāng	香	hoeng¹	liáng	涼	loeng⁴
zhāng	張	zoeng¹	chàng	唱	coeng³

The ancestral language of Putonghua and Cantonese has been proven to have '-p / -t / -k' endings. While today's Putonghua has lost all of them in its evolution, Cantonese still preserves this feature. It is difficult to tell which Putonghua finals correspond to Cantonese '-p / -t / -k' finals, but there are some clues. For example, words with short vowels such as '-i' or '-u' and pronounced in the Putonghua 2nd or 4th tone may correspond to '-p / -t / -k' in Cantonese. Putonghua '-ie' and '-üe' finals may also correspond to Cantonese '-p / -t / -k' finals. Unfortunately, in both cases, there are exceptions!

(Track 182)

shí	十	sap^6	dié	碟	dip^6
rì	日	jat^6	yuè	月	jyut^6
fú	服	fuk^6	xué	學	hok^6

9.5 Supplementary Vocabulary

9.5.1 Human body *(Track 183)*

No.	Cantonese Romanization	Chinese	Putonghua Romanization	English
1.	ji^5 • zai^2	耳仔	ěrduo 耳朵	ear
2.	ngaan^5	眼	yǎnjing 眼睛	eye
3.	goek^3	腳	jiǎo 脚 / tuǐ 腿	foot / leg
4.	sau^2	手	shǒu 手	hand
5.	tau^4	頭	tóu 头	head
6.	hau^2 / zeoi^2	口 / 嘴	zuǐba 嘴巴	mouth
7.	geng^2	頸	bózi 脖子	neck
8.	bei^6 • go^1	鼻哥	bízi 鼻子	nose
9.	bok^3 • tau^4	膊頭	jiānbǎng 肩膀	shoulder
10.	ngaa^4	牙	yáchǐ 牙齿	teeth

9.5.2 Minor illnesses *(Track 184)*

No.	Cantonese Romanization	Chinese	Putonghua Romanization	English
1.	man^5 • gam^2	敏感	mǐngǎn 敏感	allergy
2.	bui^3 • zik^3 tung^3	背脊痛	bèitòng 背痛	backache

3.	kat1	咳	késou 咳嗽	cough
4.	o1	屙	lā dùzi 拉肚子	diarrhea
5.	tau4 • wan4	頭暈	tóuyùn 头晕	dizziness
6.	sik6 • mat6 zung3 • duk6	食物中毒	shíwù zhòngdú 食物中毒	food poisoning
7.	nau2 • can1	扭親	niǔshāng 扭伤	sprain
8.	wai6 • tung3	胃痛	wèitòng 胃痛	stomachache
9.	ngaa4 • tung3	牙痛	yáteng 牙痛	toothache
10.	au2	嘔	ǒutù 呕吐	vomit

9.5.3 Medical treatment *(Track 185)*

No.	Cantonese Romanization	Chinese	Putonghua Romanization	English
1.	zam1 • gau3	針灸	zhēnjiǔ 针灸	acupuncture
2.	caa4 joek6 • gou1	搽藥膏	cā yàogāo 擦药膏	apply ointment
3.	daa2 • zam1	打針	dǎ zhēn 打针	injection
4.	on3 • mo1	按摩	ànmó 按摩	massage
5.	mat6 • lei5 zi6 • liu4	物理治療	wùlǐ zhìliáo 物理治疗	physiotherapy
6.	sik6 zung1 • joek6	食中藥	chī zhōngyào 吃中药	take Chinese medicine
7.	sik6 joek6 • seoi2	食藥水	chī yàoshuǐ 吃药水	take medicine syrup
8.	sik6 joek6 • jyun2	食藥丸	chī yàowán 吃药丸	take pills

9.5.4 Weather *(Track 186)*

No.	Cantonese Romanization	Chinese	Putonghua Romanization	English
1.	hung1 • hei3 wu1 • jim5	空氣污染	kōngqì wūrǎn 空气污染	air pollution
2.	jam1 • tin1	陰天	tiān yīn 天阴	cloudy day
3.	gon1	乾	gānzào 干燥	dry
4.	daai6 • mou6	大霧	dà wù 大雾	foggy
5.	sim2 • din6	閃電	shǎndiàn 闪电	lightning
6.	lok6 • jyu5	落雨	xià yǔ 下雨	raining

7.	hou^{2} • tin^{1}	好天	tiān qíng 天晴	sunny day
8.	haang^{4} • leoi^{4}	行雷	xíng léi 行雷	thunder
9.	daa^{2} • fung^{1} / toi^{4} • fung^{1}	打風 / 颱風	guā táifēng 刮台风	typhoon
10.	daai^{6} • fung^{1}	大風	guā dàfēng 刮大风	windy

9.6 Exercise

9.6.1 Matching

1. faat^{3} • siu^{1} 發燒 ______ A. headache
2. hau^{4} • lung^{4} tung^{3} 喉嚨痛 ______ B. running nose
3. tau^{4} • tung^{3} 頭痛 ______ C. sneezing
4. lau^{4} bei^{6} • tai^{3} 流鼻涕 ______ D. sore throat
5. daa^{2} hat^{1} • ci^{1} 打乞嗤 ______ E. fever

9.6.2 Multiple choice

1. *Do you need to see the doctor?*

   Nei^{5} 你 __________ tai^{2} 睇 ji^{1} • sang^{1} 醫生 aa^{3} 呀？

   A. jiu^{3} 要 B. tai^{2} 睇 C. sai^{2} m^{4} • sai^{2} 駛唔駛

2. *The dim sum I ate yesterday tasted very good.*

   __________ kam^{4} • jat^{6} 琴日 sik^{6} 食 __________ hou^{2} 好 hou^{2} • sik^{6} 好食。

   A. Ngo^{5} 我 …… ge^{3} dim^{2} • sam^{1} 嘅點心 B. dim^{2} • sam^{1} ge^{3} 點心嘅 …… ngo^{5} 我 C. Ngo^{5} ge^{3} 我嘅 …… dim^{2} • sam^{1} 點心

3. *Since I have a sore throat, I can't speak.*

   __________ ngo^{5} 我 hau^{4} • lung^{4} 喉嚨 tung^{3} 痛，__________ m^{4} 唔 gong^{2} • dak^{1} 講得 je^{5} 嘢。

   A. mou^{5} 冇 …… gam^{3} 咁 B. seoi^{1} • jin^{4} 雖然 …… daan^{6} • hai^{6} 但係 C. jan^{1} • wai^{6} 因為 …… so^{2} • ji^{5} 所以

4. *Although I am sick, I have to work overtime.*

_________ ngo5 我 beng6 • zo2 病咗，_________ zung6 仲 jiu3 要 hoi1 • ou1 • ti1 開OT。

A. mou5 冇 ...... gam3 咁　　B. seoi1 • jin4 雖然 ...... daan6 • hai6 但係　　C. jan1 • wai6 因為 ...... so2 • ji5 所以

5. *She is not as beautiful as her mother.*

Keoi5 佢 _________ maa4 • maa1 媽媽 _________ leng3 靚。

A. mou5 冇 ...... gam3 咁　　B. seoi1 • jin4 雖然 ...... daan6 • hai6 但係　　C. jan1 • wai6 因為 ...... so2 • ji5 所以

9.6.3 Translation

Please translate the following English / Putonghua sentences into Cantonese (Jyutping):

1. *I only have one hundred dollars.*
我有一百块而已。

____

2. *Although he has lots of money, he has no friends.*
雖然他有很多錢，但是沒有朋友。

____

3. *As I am not feeling well, I want to leave early.*
我因为不舒服，所以想先走啦。

____

4. *Among the four seasons, I like winter most.*
一年四季，我最喜欢冬天。

____

5. *Someone has already paid for you, you don't need to pay.*
有人已經幫你付款了，你不需要付款了。

____

10

Hai^{2} Hoeng^{1} • gong^{2} waan^{2}

喺香港玩 *Having fun in Hong Kong*

Learning Tasks

- to talk about one's family
- to ask and indicate the professions
- to know the tourist attractions in Hong Kong
- to plan one's trip in Hong Kong
- to know the places for dining and shopping in Hong Kong
- to end a conversation

Grammar Notes

- '*if...then...*': jyu^{4} • gwo^{2} 如果 + condition + zau^{6} 就 + consequence
- '*A the same as B*': *A* tung^{4} 同 *B* jat^{1} • joeng^{6} 一樣 + (gam^{3} 咁 + adj)
- '*A different from B*': *A* tung^{4} 同 *B* m^{4} 唔 tung^{4} 同
- ask about a person's profession: zou^{6} bin^{1} hong^{4} 做邊行
- '*before*': ji^{5} • cin^{4} 以前
- '*before and after an event / action*': ... zi^{1} • cin^{4} 之前，... zi^{1} • hau^{6} 之後
- '*ordinal numbers*': dai^{4} 第 + number
- '*finish doing something*': verb + jyun^{4} 完

Sounds and Tones

- Sounds and Tones: cross-referential tonal practice between Putonghua and Cantonese.

Supplementary Vocabulary

- scenic spots
- shopping districts
- professions
- popular foods in Hong Kong

Exercise

- matching
- fill in the blanks
- translation

 10.1 Vocabulary *(Track 187)*

No.	Cantonese Romanization	Cantonese Characters	Putonghua & Chinese Characters	English
1.	a) tai^{2} • dou^{2}	睇倒	kàndao 看到	can see
	b) tai^{2} • haa^{5}	睇吓	kànkan 看看	take a look
2.	a) soeng^{2*}	相	zhàopiàn 照片	photo
	b) uk^{1} • kei^{2*} • jan^{4} ge^{3} soeng^{2*}	屋企人嘅相	jiārén de zhàopiàn 家人的照片	family photo
3.	hau^{6} • saang^{1}	後生	niánqīng 年轻	young
4.	jyu^{4} • gwo^{2} … zau^{6} …	如果…就	rúguǒ … jiù … 如果…就…	if … then
5.	teng^{1} • dou^{2}	聽倒	tīngdao 听到	heard
6.	jat^{1} • ding^{6} hoi^{1} • sam^{1} • sei^{2} laa^{3}	一定開心死啦	yídìng kāixīn sǐle 一定开心死了	extremely happy
7.	ji^{5} • ging^{1} sei^{2} • zo^{2}	已經死咗	yǐjīng qùshì 已经去世	already passed away
8.	a) maa^{1} • saang^{1}	孖生	shuāngbāotāi 双胞胎	twins
	b) maa^{1} • saang^{1} go^{4*} • go^{1}	孖生哥哥	shuāngbāotāi gēgē 双胞胎哥哥	twins elder brother
9.	joeng^{2*}	樣	yàngzi 样子	face, look
10.	tung^{4} … jat^{1} • joeng^{6}	同…一樣	gēn … yíyàng … 跟…一样	not the same as
11.	tung^{4} … m^{4} tung^{4}	同…唔同	gēn … bù yíyàng …跟…不一样	the same as
12.	duk^{6}	讀	niàn 唸	study
13.	zung^{1} • hok^{6}	中學	zhōngxué 中学	secondary school
14.	… zi^{1} • cin^{4}	…之前	… yǐqián 以前	before an action / event
15.	… zi^{1} • hau^{6}	…之後	… yǐhòu 以后	after an action / event
16.	a) git^{3} • zo^{2} fan^{1} mei^{6} aa^{3}?	結咗婚未呀？	jiéhūnle méiyǒu? 结婚了没有？	are you married?

	b) git^{3} • zo^{2} fan^{1}	結咗婚	jiéhūnle 结婚了	married
	c) zung^{6} mei^{6} git^{3} • fan^{1}	仲未結婚	hái méiyǒu jiéhūn 还没有结婚	not married yet
17.	siu^{2} • pang^{4} • jau^{5} / sai^{3} • man^{1} • zai^{2} / sai^{3} • lou^{6} • zai^{2}	小朋友 / 細蚊仔 / 細路仔	háizi 孩子 / xiǎoháizi 小孩子	small children
18.	nei^{5} zou^{6} bin^{1} hong^{4}	你做邊行	nǐ zuò nǎ yì hang 你做哪一行	what's your profession?
19.	ji^{1} • sang^{1}	醫生	yīshēng 医生	doctor
20.	leot^{6} • si^{1}	律師	lǜshī 律师	lawyer
21.	ji^{5} • cin^{4}	以前	yǐqián 以前	before
22.	sei^{3} jat^{6} saam^{1} je^{6}	四日三夜	sì tiān sān wǎn 四天三晚	four day three night (trip)
23.	tai^{2} fung^{1} • ging^{2}	睇風景	kàn fēngjǐng 看风景	sightseeing
24.	ceoi^{4} • bin^{2*}	隨便	suíbiàn 随便	as you choose
25.	maai^{5} • haa^{5} je^{5}	買吓嘢	mǎimai dōngxi 买买东西	do some shopping
26.	sik^{6} di^{1} hou^{2} • je^{5}	食啲好嘢	chī diǎn hǎochī de 吃点好吃的	eat some good food
27.	a) dai^{6} - jat^{1}	第一	dì-yī 第一	the first
	b) dai^{6} - jat^{1} jat^{6}	第一日	dì-yī tiān 第一天	the first day
28.	Cin^{2} • seoi^{2} Waan^{1}	淺水灣	Qiǎnshuǐwān 浅水湾	Repulse Bay
29.	Hoi^{2} • joeng^{4} Gung^{1} • jyun^{2*}	海洋公園	Hǎiyánggōngyuán 海洋公园	Ocean Park
30.	Cek^{3} • cyu^{5}	赤柱	Chìzhù 赤柱	Stanley
31.	a) Sing^{1} • gwong^{1} Daai^{6} • dou^{6}	星光大道	Xīngguāngdàdào 星光大道	Avenue of Stars
	b) heoi^{3} Sing^{1} • gwong^{1} Daai^{6} • dou^{6} tai^{2} gik^{1} • gwong^{1} biu^{2} • jin^{2}	去星光大道睇激光表演	dào Xīngguāngdàdào kàn jīguāng biǎoyǎn 到星光大道看激光表演	go to the Avenue of Stars to watch laser performance

32.	jyun4	完	wán 完	finish
33.	Saan1 • deng2	山頂	Shāndǐng 山顶	the Peak
34.	Zung1 • waan4 Laan4 • gwai3 • fong1	中環蘭桂坊	Zhōnghuán Lánguìfāng 中环兰桂坊	Lan Kai Fong at Central
35.	Tung4 • lo4 • waan1 haang4 • gaai1	銅鑼灣行街	Tóngluówān guàng jiē 坐电车去铜锣湾逛街	go to Causeway Bay to stroll around
36.	nei5 • dei6 waan2 • dak1 hoi1 • sam1 di1	你哋玩得開心啲	xīwàng nǐmen wánrde kāixīn 希望你们玩得开心	hope you enjoy yourself

 10.2 Tai-Lung and Ka-Man talk about their family *(Track 188)*

Kam4 • jat6 ngo5 hai2 *Facebook* tai2 • dou2 nei5 maa4* • maa1 tung4 mui4* • mui2* ge3 soeng2*, nei5 maa4* • maa1 hou2 hau6 • saang1 aa3.
琴日我喺Facebook睇倒你媽媽同妹妹嘅相，你媽媽好後生呀。
Yesterday I saw photos of your mom's and sister's on Facebook. Your mom looks very young.
昨天我在Facebook看到你妈妈和妹妹的照片。你妈妈很年轻。

Jyu4 • gwo2 keoi5 teng1 • dou2, zau6 jat1 ding6 hoi1 • sam1 • sei2 laa3.
如果佢聽倒，就一定開心死啦。
If she heard that, she'd be thrilled.
如果她听到，就一定开心死了。

Nei5 uk1 • kei2* zung6 jau5 di1 me1 jan4 aa3?
你屋企仲有啲咩人呀？
Who else are in your family?
你家还有些哪些人？

Ngo5 baa4* • baa1 ji5 • ging1 gwo3 • zo2 • san1 laa3, uk1 • kei2* jau5 saam1 go3 jan4* ze1*. Gam2, nei5 uk1 • kei2* ne1?
我爸爸已經過咗身喇，屋企有三個人啫。噉，你屋企呢？
My father has passed away. It's just us three now. And you?
我爸爸已经去世了，家里只有三个人。那，你家呢？

Bei2 nei5 tai2 • haa5 ngo5 uk1 • kei2* • jan4 ge3 soeng2 laa1.
俾你睇吓我屋企嘅相啦。
Let me show you my family photo.
给你看看我家人的照片吧。

Tai-Lung shows Ka-Man a picture of his family stored on his iPhone.

Tai2 • haa5, ngo5 baa4* • baa1, maa4* • maa1, ze4* • ze1*, tung4 maa1 • saang1 go4* • go1.
睇吓，我爸爸、媽媽、姐姐同孖生哥哥。
Look, my father, my mother,my elder sister and my twin elder brother.
看看，我爸爸、妈妈、姐姐和双胞胎哥哥。

Maa1 • saang1? Nei5 go4* • go1 ge3 joeng2* tung4 nei5 hou2 m4 tung4 wo3.
孖生？你哥哥嘅樣同你好唔同喎。
Twins? Your elder brother doesn't look like you at all.
双胞胎？你哥哥的样子跟你很不一样。

Ngo5 • dei6 duk6 zung1 • hok6 zi1 • cin4 go3 joeng2* jat1 • joeng6, daan6 • hai6 duk6 zung1 • hok6 zi1 • hau6 zau6 m4 tung4 laa3.
我哋讀中學之前個樣一樣，但係讀中學之後就唔同喇。
Before we went to high school, we looked identical, but after that we started to look different.
我们上中学以前的样子一模一样，但是上了中学以后就不同了。

Nei5 ze4* • ze1* git3 • zo2 fan1 mei6 aa3?
你姐姐結咗婚未呀？
Has your elder sister got married yet?
你姐姐结婚了没有？

Git3 • zo2 laa3. Keoi5 ji5 • ging1 jau5 loeng5 go3 siu2 • pang4 • jau5 laa3.
結咗喇。佢已經有兩個小朋友喇。
Yes, she has. She's already got two children.
结婚了。她们已经有两个孩子。

Nei5 baa4* • baa1 maa4* • maa1 zou6 bin1 hong4 gaa3?
你爸爸媽媽做邊行㗎？
What do your dad and mom do?
你爸爸妈妈做哪一个行业的？

Ngo5 baa4* • baa1 hai6 ji1 • sang1, ngo5 maa4* • maa1 hai6 leot6 • si1.
我爸爸係醫生，我媽媽係律師。
My dad is a doctor, and my mom is a lawyer.
我爸爸是医生，我妈妈是律师。

Keoi5 • dei6 ji5 • cin4 jau5 mou5 lei4 • gwo3 Hoeng1 • gong2 aa3?
佢 哋 以 前 有 冇 嚟 過 香 港 呀 ？
Have they come to Hong Kong before?
他们以前有没有来过香港？

Mou5 aa3, daan6 • hai6 ngo5 maa4* • maa1 tung4 go4* • go1 haa6 go3 jyut6 wui5 lei4 waan2.
冇 呀 ， 但 係 我 媽 媽 同 哥 哥 下 個 月 會 嚟 玩 。
No, but my mom and elder brother will come have some fun next month.
没有，但是我妈妈跟哥哥下个月会来玩。

Nei5 jat1 • ding6 hou2 hoi1 • sam1 laak3!
你 一 定 好 開 心 嘞 ！
You must be so happy.
你一定很高兴吧！

Seoi1 • jin4 hoi1 • sam1, daan6 • hai6 m4 • zi1 daai3 keoi5 • dei6 heoi3 bin1 • dou6 waan2. Hai6 laa3! Nei5 ho2 m4 ho2 • ji5 bong1 ngo5 aa3?
雖 然 開 心 ， 但 係 唔 知 帶 佢 哋 去 邊 度 玩 。
係 喇 ！ 你 可 唔 可 以 幫 我 呀 ？
I am, but I don't know where I should take them to have some fun. Oh yes, I wonder if you could help me.
虽然高兴，但是不知道带他们上哪儿玩。对了！你能帮我吗？

Keoi5 • dei6 wui5 hai2 Hoeng1 • gong2 gei2 • do1 jat6 aa3?
佢 哋 會 喺 香 港 幾 多 日 呀 ？
How many days will they be staying in Hong Kong?
他们会在香港待几天？

Sei3 jat6 saam1 je6.
四 日 三 夜 。
Four days and three nights.
四天三夜。

Keoi5 • dei6 jiu3 lei4 maai5 • je5 ding6 tai2 fung1 • ging2 aa3?
佢 哋 要 嚟 買 嘢 定 係 睇 風 景 呀 ？
Are they coming for shopping or for sightseeing?
他们要来购物还是看风景？

Keoi5 • dei6 ceoi4 • bin2* tai2 • haa5, maai5 • haa5 je5, sik6 di1 hou2 • je5 zau6 dak1 gaa3 laa3.
佢 哋 隨 便 睇 吓 、 買 吓 嘢 、 食 啲 好 嘢 就 得 㗎 喇 。
They just want to look around, do some shopping, and eat some good food. That's all.
他们只是想随便看看、买买东西、吃点好吃的就成了。

Bat1 • jyu4 dai6-jat1 jat6 heoi3 Cin2 • seoi2 Waan1 tung4 Hoi2 • joeng4 Gung1 • jyun2* waan2 • haa5 sin1, gan1 • zyu6 heoi3 Cek3 • cyu5 maai5 • je5.
不如第一日去淺水灣同海洋公園玩吓先，跟住去赤柱買嘢。
On the first day, why not go to Repulse Bay and Ocean Park to have some fun first, then go to Stanley for some shopping.
第一天，去浅水湾和海洋公园玩一玩，然后去赤柱买东西吧。

Hou2 aa3! Hai2 Gau2 • lung4 jau5 me1 dei6 • fong1 hou2 • waan2 aa3?
好呀！喺九龍有咩地方好玩呀？
Sounds good. What places are fun in Kowloon?
好哇！在九龙有什么好玩儿的地方吗？

Hai2 Wong6 • gok3 sik6 dim2 • sam1 sin1, gan1 • zyu6 heoi3 Zim1 • saa1 • zeoi2 maai5 • je5, je6 • maan5 heoi3 Sing1 • gwong1 Daai6 • dou6 tai2 gik1 • gwong1 biu2 • jin2.
喺旺角食點心先，跟住去尖沙咀買嘢，夜晚去星光大道睇激光表演。
Have dim sum in Mong Kok first, then go to Tsim Sha Tsui for some shopping. Go to the Avenue of Stars to watch the laser performance at night.
先在旺角吃点心，然后去尖沙嘴买东西，晚上到星光大道看激光表演。

Dou1 hou2 aa1! Ngo5 maa4* • maa1 soeng2 heoi3 Saan1 • deng2, heoi3 • jyun4 Saan1 • deng2, zung6 ho2 • ji5 heoi3 bin1 • dou6 aa3?
都好吖！我媽媽想去山頂。去完山頂，仲可以去邊度呀？
That sounds good, too. My mom wants to go to the Peak. Where else can we go after the Peak?
也挺好！我妈妈想去山顶。去完山顶，还可以去哪儿？

Hai2 Saan1 • deng2 tai2 • jyun4 fung1 • ging2, ho2 • ji5 heoi3 Laan4 • gwai3 • fong1 sik6 • faan6 waak6 • ze2 heoi3 Tung4 • lo4 • waan1 haang4 • gaai1.
喺山頂睇完風景，可以去蘭桂坊食飯或者去銅鑼灣行街。
When you've finished enjoying the view from the Peak, you can go to Lan Kwai Fong for a meal or go to Causeway Bay for a stroll.
在山顶看完风景，可以去兰桂坊吃饭或者去铜锣湾逛逛。

M4 • goi1 • saai3 nei5 aa3! Dai6 • jat6 ceng2 nei5 sik6 • faan6 laa1.
唔該晒你呀！第日請你食飯啦！
Thank you so much. Our next meal together is on me.
太谢了！改天我请你做客。

Do^{1} • ze^{6} sin^{1}, nei^{5} • dei^{6} waan^{2} • dak^{1} hoi^{1} • sam^{1} di^{1} laa^{1}.
多 謝 先 ， 你 哋 玩 得 開 心 啲 啦 。
Thanks. Hope you guys will enjoy yourselves.
先谢了，希望你们玩得开心。

10.3 Grammar Notes

10.3.1 '*If … then …*': jyu^{4} • gwo^{2} 如果 + condition + zau^{6} 就 + consequence

(Track 189)

"Jyu^{4} • gwo^{2} 如果 + X, zau^{6} 就 + Y" is used to mean *if X, then Y.* "Jyu^{4} • gwo^{2} 如果" can be used as a conditional or counterfactual clause. "Zau^{6} 就" has to be placed between the subject and the verb as in example 2.

P rúguǒ 如果 … jiù 就 …

Examples:

1. Jyu^{4} • gwo^{2} ngo^{5} jau^{5} • cin^{2*}, zau^{6} hou^{2} hoi^{1} • sam^{1}.
   如 果 我 有 錢 ， 就 好 開 心 。
   If I had money, I'd be very happy.
   如果我有钱，就很高兴。

2. Jyu^{4} • gwo^{2} nei^{5} heoi^{3}, ngo^{5} zau^{6} heoi^{3}.
   如 果 你 去 ， 我 就 去 。
   If you go, then I'll go.
   如果你去，我就去。

10.3.2 '*The same as* A': tung^{4} 同 + A + jat^{1} • joeng^{6} 一樣 + (gam^{3} 咁 + adj)

(Track 190)

"Tung^{4} 同 + A + jat^{1} • joeng^{6} 一樣" is used for comparison of equality. This phrase can go on with "gam^{3} 咁 + adj" to express in what way two items are similar, corresponding to "*as* … *as* adj" in English.

P gēn 跟 + A + yíyàng 一样 (+ adj)

Examples:

1. Nei^{5} tung^{4} ji^{5} • cin^{4} jat^{1} • joeng^{6}, dou^{1} • hai^{6} gam^{3} leng^{3}.
   你 同 以 前 一 樣 ， 都 係 咁 靚 。
   You are just like before, still so beautiful.
   你跟以前一样，还是那么亮丽。

2. Dik^{6} • si^{6} • nei^{4} tung^{4} Hoi^{2} • joeng^{4} Gung^{1} • jyun^{2*} jat^{1} • joeng^{6} gam^{3} hou^{2} • waan^{2}.
迪 士 尼 同 海 洋 公 園 一 樣 咁 好 玩 。
Disneyland is as enjoyable as Ocean Park.
迪斯尼跟海洋公园一样好玩。

10.3.3 '*Different from* A': tung^{4} 同 A m^{4} 唔 tung^{4} 同 (Track 191)

"Tung^{4} 同 + A + m^{4} 唔 tung^{4} 同" denotes something or somebody is '*different from A*'.

P gēn 跟 + A + bù yíyàng 不一样

Examples:

1. *Peter* tung^{4} ngo^{5} m^{4} tung^{4}. Keoi^{5} sik^{1} gong^{2} Gwong^{2} • dung^{1} • waa^{2*}, ngo^{5} m^{4} sik^{1}.
Peter 同 我 唔 同 。 佢 識 講 廣 東 話 ， 我 唔 識 。
Peter is different from me. He speaks Cantonese, but I can't.
Peter 跟我不一样。他会说广东话，我不会。

2. Keoi^{5} tung^{4} ji^{5} • cin^{4} m^{4} tung^{4}, fei^{4} • zo^{2} hou^{2} do^{1}.
佢 同 以 前 唔 同 ， 肥 咗 好 多 。
She is different from before, she gained a bit of weight.
她跟以前不一样，胖了很多。

10.3.4 Ask someone's profession: zou^{6} bin^{1} hong^{4} 做邊行 (Track 192)

"Zou^{6} bin^{1} hong^{4} 做邊行" is used to ask about a person's profession. There is a similar expression: "zou^{6} sing^{6} hong^{4} 做盛行", which is probably a little old-fashioned, but is still used occasionally.

P zuò nǎ yí ge hángyè de 做哪一个行业的？

Examples:

1. *A:* Nei^{5} zou^{6} bin^{1} hong^{4} aa^{3}?
你 做 邊 行 呀 ？
What's your profession?
你是做哪一个行业的？

B: Ngo^{5} zou^{6} lou^{5} • si^{1}.
我 做 老 師 。
I am a teacher.
我当老师。

2. *A:* Nei^{5} zou^{6} sing^{6} hong^{4} aa^{3}?
你 做 盛 行 呀 ？
What's your profession?
你是做哪一个行业的？

B: Ngo^{5} hai^{6} gung^{1} • cing^{4} • si^{1}.
我 係 工 程 師 。
I am an engineer.
我是工程师。

10.3.5 '*Before*' : ji5 • cin4 以前 *(Track 193)*

"Ji5 • cin4 以前" means '*before*' or '*formerly*'.

P yǐqián 以前

Examples:

1. Ji5 • cin4 ngo5 hai2 zing3 • fu2 zou6 • je5.
   以 前 我 喺 政 府 做 嘢 。
   I was formerly a civil servant.
   以前我在政府工作。

2. Keoi5 ji5 • cin4 hai6 ngo5 tung4 • hok6, ji4 • gaa1 hai6 ngo5 naam3 pang4 • jau5.
   佢 以 前 係 我 同 學 ， 而 家 係 我 男 朋 友 。
   He was my classmate before, but now he is my boyfriend.
   她以前是我同学，现在是我男朋友。

10.3.6 '*Temporal sequence*' : "… zi1 • cin4 之前" and "… zi1 • hau6 之後" *(Track 194)*

"… zi1 • cin4 之前" (*prior to …*) and "… zi1 • hau6 之後" (*after / since …*) are used to denote the temporal sequence of actions or events. Unlike English, "… zi1 • cin4" and "… zi1 • hau6" always come before the main clause. In Putonghua, "yǐqián 以前" and "zhīqián 之前", "yǐhòu 以后" and "zhīhòu 之后" can be used interchangeably, but in Cantonese, only "… zi1 • cin4" and "… zi1 • hau6" can be used.

P … yǐqián 以前，… yǐhòu 以后

Examples:

1. Ngo5 lei4 Hoeng1 • gong2 ji1 • cin4, hai2 Bak1 • ging1 hok6 Pou2 • tung1 • waa2*.
   我 嚟 香 港 之 前 ， 喺 北 京 學 普 通 話 。
   He learned Putonghua in Beijing before he came to Hong Kong.
   我来香港之前，在北京学普通话。

2. Keoi5 git3 • fan1 zi1 • cin4 m4 sik1 zyu2 • faan6, daan6 • hai6 git3 • zo2 fan1 zi1 • hau6 zyu2 • je5 hou2 hou2 • sik6.
   佢 結 婚 之 前 唔 識 煮 飯 ， 但 係 結 咗 婚 之 後 煮 嘢 好 好 食 。
   She couldn't cook before her marriage, but she's been a good cook since she got married.
   她结婚之前不会做饭，但是结了婚之后煮东西很好吃。

10.3.7 ‘*Ordinal numbers*’: dai6 第 + number *(Track 195)*

“Dai4 第 + number” is used to express ‘*ordinal numbers*’.

P dì 第 + number

Examples:

1. Keoi5 hai6 ngo5 dai6- jat1 go3 Hoeng1 • gong2 pang4 • jau5.
   佢 係 我 第 一 個 香 港 朋 友 。
   He is my first friend in Hong Kong.
   他是我第一个香港朋友。

2. Dai6-jat1 ci3 m4 gwaan3, dai6-ji6 ci3 zau6 gwaan3 gaa3 laa3.
   第 一 次 唔 慣 ， 第 二 次 就 慣 㗎 喇 。
   You may not be used to it at the first time, but by the second time you will get used to it.
   第一次不习惯，第二次就会习惯的。

10.3.8 ‘*Finish doing something*’: verb + jyun4 完 *(Track 196)*

“Jyun4 完” is used after a verb to denote the whole process of action has finished. When the verb has an object, “jyun4” is placed between the verb and the object. It is often used to express temporal sequence: Used in the first clause, it denotes the action in the second clause occurs after the first action comes to an end, as in example 2.

P … wán 完

Examples:

1. *A:* Nei5 se2 • jyun4 bou3 • gou3 mei6 aa3?
   你 寫 完 報 告 未 呀 ？
   Have you finished writing your report?
   你写完报告了吗？

   B: Mei6 aa3.
   未 呀 。
   Not yet.
   还没有。

2. Ngo5 zou6 • jyun4 wan6 • dung6, cung1 • loeng4.
   我 做 完 運 動 ， 沖 涼 。
   I’ll take a shower after doing exercise.
   我做完运动，洗澡。

10.4 Cantonese and Putonghua tones in comparison : *(Track 197)*

Cantonese and Putonghua are genetically related. This is why we can see some connections in tonal patterns. Unlike initials and finals, tonal pitch does not show much resemblance. However, tonal class from their ancestral language is often kept in both Cantonese and Putonghua. So all you need is to remember which tone pitch pattern in Putonghua generally corresponds to which tone pitch in Cantonese, using the following table.

Putonghua		***Cantonese***		***General Rules***
Tone 1	5 4 3 2 1 	5 4 3 2 1 	**Tone 1 (high level)**	Putonghua Tone 1 generally corresponds to Cantonese Tone 1.
Tone 2	5 4 3 2 1 	5 4 3 2 1 	**Tone 4 (low falling)**	Putonghua Tone 2 generally corresponds to Cantonese Tone 4. It is a rising tone in Putonghua while it's low falling in Cantonese.
Tone 3	5 4 3 2 1 	5 4 3 2 1 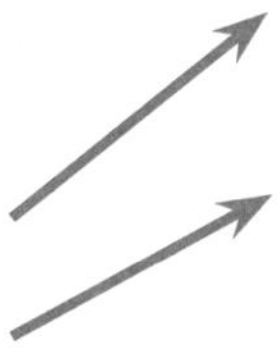	**Tone 2 (high rising)** **Tone 5 (low rising)**	Putonghua Tone 3 corresponds to either Tone 2 or Tone 5 in Cantonese. Putonghua words with finals 'l-', 'm-', 'n-', 'w-', 'y-' tend to belong to Tone 5 in Cantonese.
Tone 4	5 4 3 2 1 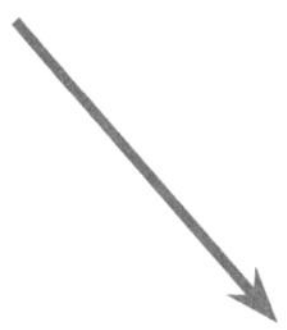	5 4 3 2 1 	**Tone 3 (mid level)** **Tone 6 (low level)**	Putonghua Tone 4 corresponds to either Tone 3 or Tone 6 in Cantonese. Putonghua words with finals 'l-', 'm-', 'n-', 'w-', 'y-' tend to belong to Tone 6 in Cantonese.

Examples:

Putonghua	Chinese characters	Cantonese	Putonghua	Chinese characters	Cantonese
xiānshēng	先生	sin^{1} • saang^{1}	zhōngxīn	中心	zung^{1} • sam^{1}
píngshí	平時	ping^{4} • si^{4}	máfán	麻煩	maa^{4} • faan^{4}
shǒuzhǐ	手指	sau^{2} • zi^{2}	xiǎojiě	小姐	siu^{2} • ze^{2}
yǒngyuǎn	永遠	wing^{5} • jyun^{5}	mǔyǔ	母語	mou^{5} • jyu^{5}
zàijiàn	再見	zoi^{3} • gin^{3}	bànjià	半價	bun^{3} • gaa^{3}
nèidì	內地	noi^{6} • dei^{6}	yùndòng	運動	wan^{6} • dung^{6}

†† N.B.: The above rules cannot be applied to tones of Cantonese words that end with -p, -t, -k.

10.5 Supplementary Vocabulary

10.5.1 Scenic spots *(Track 198)*

No.	Cantonese Romanization	Chinese	Putonghua Romanization	English
1.	Jat^{1} • baat^{3} • baat^{3} • jat^{1}	1881	Yībābāyī 1881	1881 Heritage
2.	Zoek^{3} • niu^{5} Faa^{1} • jyun^{2*}	雀鳥花園	Quèniǎo huāyuán 雀鸟花园	Bird Garden
3.	Tin^{1} • taan^{4} daai^{6} • fat^{6}	天壇大佛	Tiāntán dàfó 天坛大佛	Giant Buddha
4.	Paau^{2} • maa^{5} • dei^{2*}	跑馬地	Pǎomǎdì 跑马地	Happy Valley Racecourse
5.	Sap^{1} • dei^{6} Gung^{1} • jyun^{2*}	濕地公園	Shīdì gōngyuán 香港湿地公园	Hong Kong Wetland Park
6.	Zan^{1} • bou^{2} Wong^{4} • gwok^{3}	珍寶王國	Zhēnbǎo wángguó 珍宝王国	Jumbo Kingdom
7.	Mei^{5} • lei^{6} • lau^{4}	美利樓	Měilìlóu 美利楼	Murray House
8.	Ngong^{4} • ping^{4} saam^{1} • luk^{6} • ling^{4}	昂坪 360	Ángpíng 360 昂坪 360	Ngong Ping 360
9.	Miu^{2*} • gaai^{1}	廟街	Miàojiē 庙街	Temple Street
10.	Wong^{4} • daai^{6} • sin^{1}	黃大仙	Huángdàxiān 黄大仙	Wong Tai Sin Temple

10.5.2 Shopping districts *(Track 199)*

No.	Cantonese Romanization	Chinese	Putonghua Romanization	English
1.	Jyun^{4} • fong^{1}	圓方	Yuánfāng 圆方	Elements
2.	Jau^{6} • jat^{1} • sing^{4}	又一城	Yòuyìchéng 又一城	Fashion Walk
3.	Hoi^{2} • gong^{2} Sing^{4}	海港城	Hǎigǎngchéng 海港城	Harbor City
4.	Gwok^{3} • zai^{3} gam^{1} • jung^{4} zung^{1} • sam^{1}	國際金融中心	Guójì jīnróng Zhōngxīn 国际金融中心	International Finance Centre
5.	Long^{5} • hou^{4} • fong^{1}	朗豪坊	Lǎngháofāng 朗豪坊	Langham Place
6.	San^{1} sing^{4} • si^{5} Gwong^{2} • coeng^{4}	新城市廣場	Xīnchéngshì guǎngchǎng 新城市广场	New Town Plaza
7.	Taai^{3} • gu^{2} Gwong^{2} • coeng^{4}	太古廣場	Tàigǔ guǎngchǎng 太古广场	Pacific Place

8.	Sung^4 • gwong^1 Baak^3 • fo^3	崇光百貨	Chóngguāng bǎihuò 崇光百货	Sogo
9.	Zi^3 • dei^6 Gwong^2 • coeng^4	置地廣場	Zhìdì guǎngchǎng 置地广场	The Landmark
10.	Si^4 • doi^6 Gwong^2 • coeng^4	時代廣場	Shídài guǎngchǎng 时代广场	Times Square

10.5.3 Professions *(Track 200)*

No.	Cantonese Romanization	Chinese	Putonghua Romanization	English
1.	wui^6 • gai^3 • si^1	會計師	kuàijìshī 会计师	accountant
2.	man^4 • jyun^4	文員	wényuán 文员	clerk
3.	si^1 • gei^1	司機	sījī 司机	chauffeur
4.	bou^2 • him^2 ging^1 • gei^2	保險經紀	bǎoxiǎn jīngjì 保险经纪	insurance agent
5.	ging^1 • lei^5	經理	jīnglǐ 经理	manager
6.	ging^2 • caat^3	警察	jǐngchá 警察	policeman
7.	jau^4 • caai^1	郵差	yóuchāi 邮差	postman
8.	sau^6 • fo^3 • jyun^4	售貨員	shòuhuòyuán 售货员	salesclerk
9.	lou^5 • si^1	老師	lǎoshī 老师	teacher
10.	gung^1 • jan^4	工人	gōngrén 工人	domestic helper / worker

10.5.4 Popular foods in Hong Kong *(Track 201)*

No.	Cantonese Romanization	Chinese	Putonghua Romanization	English
1.	Bak^1 • ging^1 coi^3	北京菜	Běijīng cài 北京菜	Beijing food
2.	Gwong^2 • dung^1 coi^3	廣東菜	Guǎngdōng cài 广东菜	Cantonese food
3.	Ciu^4 • zau^1 coi^3	潮州菜	Cháozhōu cài 潮州菜	Chaozhou food
4.	Jan^3 • dou^6 coi^3	印度菜	Yìndù cài 印度菜	Indian food
5.	Jan^3 • nei^4 coi^3	印尼菜	Yìndùníxīyà cài 印度尼西亚菜	Indonesian food
6.	Jat^6 • bun^2 coi^3	日本菜	Rìběn cài 日本菜	Japanese food
7.	Hon^4 • gwok^3 coi^3	韓國菜	Hánguó cài 韩国菜	Korean food

8.	Soeng^{6} • hoi^{2} coi^{3}	上海菜	Shànghǎi cài 上海菜	Shanghainese food
9.	Taai^{3} • gwok^{3} coi^{3}	泰國菜	Tàiguó cài 泰国菜	Thai food
10.	Jyut^{6} • naam^{4} coi^{3}	越南菜	Yuènán cài 越南菜	Vietnamese food

10.6 Exercise

10.6.1 Matching

1. Laan^{4} • gwai^{3} • fong^{1} 蘭桂坊 ______ A. Ocean Park
2. Cek^{3} • cyu^{5} 赤柱 ______ B. Lan Kai Fong
3. Cin^{2} • seoi^{2} Waan^{1} 淺水灣 ______ C. the Peak
4. Hoi^{2} • joeng^{4} Gung^{1} • jyun^{2*} 海洋公園 ______ D. Stanley
5. Saan^{1} • deng^{2} 山頂 ______ E. Repulse Bay

10.6.2 Multiple choice

1. *If you need my help, you can call me.*

   ______ nei^{5} 你 jau^{5} 有 man^{6} • tai^{4} 問題，______ daa^{2} din^{6} • waa^{2*} 打電話 bei^{2} 俾 ngo^{5} 我 laa^{1} 啦。

   A. jau^{6} 就 …… jyu^{4} • gwo^{2} 如果
   B. jyu^{4} • gwo^{2} 如果 …… jau^{6} 就
   C. jyu^{4} • gwo^{2} 如果 …… hou^{2} 好

2. *My father says I can work in any profession I like.*

   Ngo^{5} 我 baa^{4*} • baa^{1} 爸爸 waa^{6} 話 ngo^{5} 我 zung^{1} • ji^{3} 鍾意 ______dou^{1} 都 dak^{1} 得。

   A. zou^{6} bin^{1} hong^{4} 做邊行
   B. bin^{1} hong^{4} zou^{6} 邊行做
   C. zou^{6} hong^{4} bin^{1} 做行邊

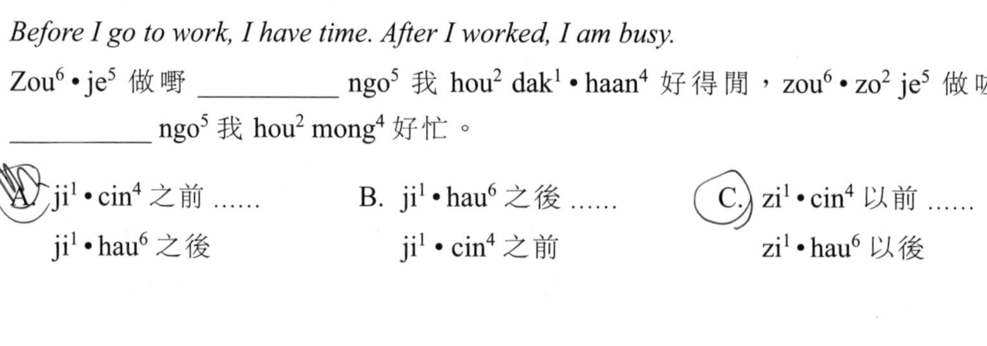

3. *Before I go to work, I have time. After I worked, I am busy.*

   Zou^{6} • je^{5} 做嘢 ______ ngo^{5} 我 hou^{2} dak^{1} • haan^{4} 好得閒，zou^{6} • zo^{2} je^{5} 做咗嘢 ______ ngo^{5} 我 hou^{2} mong^{4} 好忙。

   A. ji^{1} • cin^{4} 之前 …… ji^{1} • hau^{6} 之後
   B. ji^{1} • hau^{6} 之後 …… ji^{1} • cin^{4} 之前
   C. zi^{1} • cin^{4} 以前 …… zi^{1} • hau^{6} 以後

4. *Korean food is as tasty as Japanese food.*

Hon^4 • gwok^3 coi^3 韓國菜 __________ Jat^6 • bun^2 coi^3 日本菜 __________ gam^3 咁 hou^2 • sik^6 好食。

A. tung^4 同 ...... jat^1 • joeng^6 一樣
B. m^4 tung^4 唔同 ...... jat^1 • joeng^6 一樣
C. tung^4 同 ...... m^4 tung^4 唔同

5. *You can watch TV when you finish doing homework.*

Nei^5 你 zou^6 做 • __________ gung^1 • fo^3 功課，ho^2 • ji^5 可以 tai^2 睇 din^6 • si^6 電視。

A. gan^2 緊
B. jyun^4 完
C. zi^1 • hau^6 之後

10.6.3 Translation

Please translate the following English / Potunghua sentences into Cantonese (Jyutping):

1. *He was rich in the past.*
他以前很富有。

____

2. *Many young people in Hong Kong like to go to Langham Place for shopping.*
很多香港的年青人喜欢去朗豪坊买东西。

____

3. *Have you ever been to the Avenue of Stars to watch the laser performance?*
你有没有去过到星光大道看激光表演？

____

4. *My twin elder sister was a doctor before marriage.*
我的双胞胎姐姐在结婚以前当医生。

____

5. *This is the first time I've been to Jumbo Kingdom to eat seafood.*
这次是我第一次去珍宝王国吃海鲜。

____

Index

◇◇◇◇◇◇◇◇

Suggested answers

1. Making new friends

1.6.1

1. **C** 2. **A** 3. **E** 4. **B** 5. **D**

1.6.2

1. **B** 2. **C** 3. **C** 4. **A** 5. **A**

1.6.3

1. *Peter* hai^{6} **Gaa^{1} • naa^{4} • daai^{6}** jan^{4}, sik^{1} gong^{2} **Faat^{3} • man^{2*}** .
2. *Mary* hai^{6} **Mei^{5} • gwok^{3}** jan^{4}, sik^{1} gong^{2} **Jing^{1} • man^{2*}** .
3. *Jane* hai^{6} **Fei^{1} • leot^{6} • ban^{1}** jan^{4}, sik^{1} gong^{2} **Fei^{1} • leot^{6} • ban^{1} • waa^{2*}** .
4. *Pual* hai^{6} **Zung^{1} • gwok^{3}** jan^{4}, sik^{1} gong^{2} **Pou^{2} • tung^{1} • waa^{2*}** .

2. Lunch in the Canteen

2.6.1

1. **E** 2. **A** 3. **D** 4. **C** 5. **B**

2.62

1. **C** 2. **A** 3. **B** 4. **A** 5. **C**

2.6.3

1. **J , C , E** 2. **A , J/E** 3. **B , G** 4. **H , F** 5. **I**

3. Shopping

3.6.1

1. **E** 2. **D** 3. **A** 4. **C** 5. **B**

3.62

1. **C** 2. **B** 3. **B** 4. **A** 5. **C**

3.6.3

1. **I**	2. **C**	3. **A**	4. **G**	5. **E**
6. **H**	7. **F**	8. **J**	9. **B**	10. **D**

4. Campus life

4.6.1

1. **C**	2. **E**	3. **D**	4. **B**	5. **A**

4.6.2

1. **C**	2. **B**	3. **A**	4. **A**	5. **B**

4.6.3

1. **D , G**	2. **E , H**	3. **F , J**	4. **C , A**	5. **B , I**

5. The transport in Hong Kong

5.6.1

1. **D**	2. **E**	3. **A**	4. **C**	5. **B**

5.6.2

1. **A**	2. **C**	3. **B**	4. **C**	5. **B**

5.6.3

1. **2 – 5 – 1 – 4 – 3** 2. **3 – 2/4 – 4/2 – 1 – 5** 3. **3 – 5 – 2 – 4 – 1**
4. **2 – 1/3 – 5 – 3/1 – 4** 5. **3 – 1 – 2 – 5 – 4**

6. Making phone calls

6.6.1

1. **B**	2. **D**	3. **E**	4. **C**	5. **A**

6.6.2

1. **B**	2. **C**	3. **A**	4. **C**	5. **A**

6.6.3

1. **1 – 5 – 2 – 4 – 3** or **5 – 4 – 1 – 3 – 2** 2. **1 – 5 – 4 – 3 – 2**
3. **1 – 3 – 5 – 2 – 4** 4. **3 – 2 – 5 – 4 – 1** 5. **4 – 3 – 1 – 2 – 5**

7. Having dim sum

7.6.1

1. **C** 2. **D** 3. **B** 4. **E** 5. **A**

7.6.2

1. **C** 2. **B** 3. **A** 4. **C** 5. **A**

7.6.3

1. Ngo^{5} joek^{3} • zo^{2} Gaa^{1} • naam^{4} tung^{4} Wing^{6} • si^{1} jam^{2}• caa^{4} aa^{3}.

2. Ngo^{5} hai^{2} Zung^{1} • waan^{4} dei^{6} • tit^{3} •zaam^{6} Hang^{4} • sang^{1} ngan^{4} • hong^{4} cin^{4} • min^{6} dang^{2} keoi^{5} • dei^{6} sin^{1}.

3. Wing^{6} • si^{1} mou^{5} lei^{4}.

4. Go^{2} • dou^{6} di^{1} haa^{1} • gaau^{2} tung^{4} siu^{1} • maai^{2*} hou^{2} hou^{2} • sik^{6}.

5. Ngo^{5} tung^{4} Gaa^{1} • naam^{4} daap^{3} din^{6} • ce^{1} heoi^{3} tai^{2} hei^{3}.

8. Karaoke

8.6.1

1. **C** 2. **E** 3. **A** 4. **B** 5. **D**

8.6.2

1. **B** 2. **B** 3. **A** 4. **C** 5. **B**

8.6.3

1. *Jane* zung^{1} • ji^{3} tai^{2} • hei^{3}.

2. *Peter* zung^{1} • ji^{3} zou^{6} wan^{6} • dung^{6} tung^{4} soeng^{5} • mong^{5}.

3. *Mary* zung^{1} • ji^{3} zou^{6} wan^{6} • dung^{6} tung^{4} maai^{5} • je^{5}.

4. *Paul* me^{1} jyu^{4} • lok^{6} dou^{1} m^{4} zung^{1} • ji^{3}.

5. Ngo^{5} dak^{1} • haan^{4} zung^{1} • ji^{3}...... .

9. Not feeling well

9.6.1

1. **E**   2. **D**   3. **A**   4. **B**   5. **C**

9.6.2

1. **C**   2. **A**   3. **C**   4. **B**   5. **A**

9.6.3

1. Ngo^{5} jau^{5} jat^{1} • baak^{3} man^{1} ze^{1}.
2. Seoi^{1} • jin^{4} keoi^{5} jau^{5} hou^{2} do^{1} cin^{2*}, daan^{6} • hai^{6} mou^{5} pang^{4} • jau^{5}.
3. Jan^{1} • wai^{6} ngo^{5} m^{4} syu^{1} • fuk^{6}, so^{2} • ji^{5} soeng^{2} zau^{2} sin^{1}.
4. Jat^{1} • nin^{4} sei^{1} gwai^{3} ngo^{5} zeoi^{3} zung^{1} • ji^{3} cau^{1} • tin^{1}.
5. Jau^{5} jan^{4} bong^{1} nei^{5} bei^{2} • jo^{2} cin^{2*}, (*nei^{5}) m^{4} • sai^{2} bei^{2} laa^{3}.

10. Not feeling well

10.6.1

1. **B**   2. **D**   3. **E**   4. **A**   5. **C**

10.6.2

1. **B**   2. **A**   3. **C**   4. **A**   5. **B**

10.6.3

1. Keoi^{5} ji^{5} • cin^{4} hou^{2} jau^{5} cin^{2*}.
2. Hou^{2} do^{1} hau^{6} • saang^{1} • zai^{2} zung^{1} • ji^{3} heoi^{3} Long^{5} • hou^{4}• fong^{1} maai^{5} je^{5}.
3. Nei^{5} jau^{5} mou^{5} heoi^{3} • gwo^{3} Sing^{1} • gwong^{1} Daai^{6} • dou^{6} tai^{2} gik^{1} • gwong^{1} biu^{2} • jin^{2} aa^{3}?
4. Ngo^{5} ge^{3} maa^{1} • saang^{1} ze^{4} • ze^{1} git^{1} • fan^{1} zi^{1} • cin^{4} zou^{6} ji^{1} • sang^{1}.
5. Ni^{1} ci^{3} hai^{6} ngo^{5} dai^{6}-jat^{1} ci^{3} heoi^{3} Zan^{1} • bou^{2} Wong^{4} • gwok^{3} sik^{6} hoi^{2} • sin^{1}.